I0625214

THE MINISTRY OF JESUS

A DEVOTIONAL CELEBRATING THE WORK,
WORDS, AND WITNESS OF CHRIST

HOLIDAY CELEBRATION DEVOTIONALS
BOOK 4

PETER DEHAAN

Library of Congress Control Number: 9798888090558

Published by Rock Rooster Books, Grand Rapids, Michigan

ISBNs:

- 979-8-88809-054-1 (e-book)
- 979-8-88809-055-8 (paperback)
- 979-8-88809-056-5 (hardcover)
- 979-8-88809-057-2 (audiobook)

Credits:

- Developmental editor: Julie Harbison
- Copyeditor: Robyn Mulder
- Cover design: Cassidy Wierks
- Author photo: Chelsie Jensen Photography

To Dave Sue

Series by Peter DeHaan

Holiday Celebration Devotionals rejoice in the holidays with Jesus.

40-Day Bible Study Series takes a fresh and practical look into Scripture, book by book.

Bible Character Sketches Series celebrates people in Scripture, from the well-known to the obscure.

Visiting Churches Series takes an in-person look at church practices and traditions to inform and inspire today's followers of Jesus.

CONTENTS

CELEBRATING THE MINISTRY OF JESUS

The "Holiday Celebration Devotionals" series looks at times when Christians gather to rejoice in their faith and praise God for who he is and what he has done. Depending on your practices and preferences, the labels used and scope of the festivities change, but in general terms, we celebrate Christmas and Easter.

We cover the Christmas season (which can include Advent and Epiphany) in the devotional book *The Advent of Jesus*. And we celebrate the Easter season (which can encompass Lent, Good Friday, Ascension Day, and Pentecost) in the devotional books *The Passion of Jesus* and *The Victory of Jesus*.

This book, *The Ministry of Jesus*, doesn't address these specific holiday seasons but instead revels in the space between them, sometimes called Ordinary Time—but there's nothing ordinary about it.

In the Christmas season, we observe the Messiah coming as a baby to save us. In the Easter season we remember the resurrected Savior who has successfully completed his mission.

The church calendar has but a few weeks between these two holy seasons, yet historically there are three decades between them: thirty-three years transpire between Jesus's birth and his resurrection from the dead.

The last three years of Jesus's life are when his ministry on earth occurs. This is what we'll cover in this devotional, which is also the bulk of what's addressed in the four biographies of Jesus in the Bible: Matthew, Mark, Luke, and John.

For our purposes, we'll use the timeline in Mark's gospel of Jesus to guide us. We'll weave in Matthew, Luke, and John as appropriate to look at Jesus's words, work, and witness.

You can use this devotional in the period between the Christmas season and the Easter season, which spans a few weeks. Or you can read it in the time after Easter and prior to Christmas, which lasts about six months. Or do both.

However you proceed, may God speak to you, inspire you, and bless you through this devotional as you immerse yourself in wonder over the ministry of Jesus and what he has done for us.

DAY 1: JOHN PREPARES THE WAY

TODAY'S PASSAGE: MARK 1:1–8, WITH
MATTHEW 3:1–12 AND LUKE 3:1–18

Focus verse: *"I baptize you with water, but he will baptize you with the Holy Spirit."* (Mark 1:8)

Our story of Jesus's ministry begins with John the Baptist. In the area around the Jordan River, John preaches a message of repentance. The people wonder if John is the one—foretold by the Old Testament prophets —who will come to save them.

He is not. John comes to prepare the way for Jesus. Mark cites two passages of Scripture that predict John the Baptist's mission and purpose. The first is from Malachi 3:1, and the second is from Isaiah 40:3. In Luke's biography of Jesus, he quotes a longer passage from Isaiah, going through to verse 5.

John acknowledges Jesus is more powerful and more important than him—much more so. The apostle doesn't even deem himself worthy to stoop to untie Jesus's sandals.

From this we get the image of a servant washing the feet of his master at the end of the day. The servant stoops to untie and remove his master's sandals. He washes the day's filth from his master's feet. The lowest of servants would handle this disgusting job.

Yet John deems himself unworthy to do even this for Jesus.

John proclaims a message of repentance to the people, urging them to acknowledge remorse over the wrong things they have done. For those who want to publicly show their repentance—committing to make a U-turn with their lives—John baptizes them.

Once they admit their guilt and receive his baptism, he urges them to change their behavior. It starts with repentance and baptism. Changing their lifestyle happens later. It's a response to their commitment.

John tells the people that he baptizes them with

water, whereas the one who will come after him—Jesus—will baptize them with the Holy Spirit. Matthew and Luke both expand on this, saying that Jesus will baptize them with the Holy Spirit *and* with fire.

All who believe in Jesus will receive baptism with the Holy Spirit (1 Corinthians 12:13). The second phrase, baptism by fire, refers to judgment. This is not judgment for those who follow Jesus, but it's judgment for those who do not.

Questions*: How should we react to the idea of Jesus baptizing us with the Holy Spirit and with fire? Is John's baptism for repentance enough (see Acts 18:24–26)?*

Prayer: Jesus, may we receive Holy Spirit baptism and follow you for the rest of our lives.

DAY 2: DO WHAT IS PROPER

TODAY'S PASSAGE: MARK 1:9–11, WITH
MATTHEW 3:13–17, LUKE 3:21–22, AND JOHN
1:29–34

Focus verse: *A voice came from heaven: "You are my
Son, whom I love; with you I am well pleased."* (Mark
1:11)

At this point, Jesus asks John to baptize
him. This seems strange because John's
message is one of repentance from sins,
and Jesus is sinless (1 John 3:5). Jesus doesn't need to
be baptized to make a public declaration that he's
repenting from the wrong things he's done. He's
done nothing wrong.

In Matthew 3, John recognizes this and objects.
The lesser should not baptize the one who is
greater. If anything, Jesus should baptize John.

John is the greatest man to ever live (Luke 7:28). But he isn't perfect. He struggles with sin the same as everyone else. Though he can't baptize himself, Jesus could. But Jesus won't. He refuses.

Jesus simply says it's proper for John to baptize him. This will fulfill all righteousness—that is, to do what is right and what is required. In this way, Jesus —while remaining sinless—demonstrates that he associates with sinners. Since we all have sinned, he identifies with us in our predicament of sinfulness.

At last, John agrees to baptize Jesus (Matthew 3:15).

Imagine what John must think as he baptizes the Messiah, a man so important that John considers himself unworthy to even unlace his sandals. John lowers Jesus into the water, the same as he's done hundreds of times for sinners who repented. But Jesus has nothing to repent from.

John lifts Jesus out of the water. This completes his public display of repentance and shows a picture of cleansing. Though this is where John's other baptisms end, it doesn't mark the end of Jesus's.

At this point, heaven opens, and God's Spirit descends. It looks like a dove and moves toward

Jesus, resting on him. This shows God's pleasure over Jesus's baptism and proves it's like no other.

Verifying this visual confirmation of Jesus's uniqueness comes an audible affirmation as well. A voice booms from heaven. "This is my Son," Father God says. "I love him so much and am most pleased with who he is and what he's done."

Now John and everyone gathered around knows that Jesus is special, that he's the Son of God. Though it will be a while before most people fully comprehend this, God confirms it to be true before Jesus starts his public ministry.

But this isn't the only time we hear the voice of God affirming Jesus. We'll cover it again in Day 30, toward the end of Jesus's ministry here on earth.

Questions*: What do we think about Jesus being baptized? Though we may have never heard the audible voice of God, in what other ways has God spoken to us?*

Prayer: Father God, when you speak to us, may we hear, listen, and obey.

DAY 3: SATAN STRIKES OUT

TODAY'S PASSAGE: MARK 1:12–13, WITH
MATTHEW 4:1–11 AND LUKE 4:1–13

Focus verse: *At once the Spirit sent [Jesus] out into the wilderness, and he was in the wilderness forty days, being tempted by Satan.* (Mark 1:12–13)

The conclusion of Jesus's baptism verifies he is the Son of God and shows that the Holy Spirit lives within him. The first thing the Holy Spirit does is prompt Jesus to go to the wilderness. There, Satan tempts Jesus for forty days.

Though Mark doesn't tell us about Jesus's temptation, Matthew and Luke do. Let's look at what happens in Luke's account.

Jesus fasts for these forty days. He eats nothing

while in the desert. His body is weak and his resolve, lessened. In case we miss the obvious, Luke says Jesus is hungry. It's now, when Jesus is at his weakest, that the devil sees his best opportunity to tempt the Savior into aborting his mission.

The devil taunts Jesus.

Capitalizing on Jesus's hunger, Satan encourages Jesus to turn a stone into a loaf of bread. Then he'll have something to eat. Performing a miracle will also confirm his power.

But Jesus doesn't fall for the enemy's trap. Jesus quotes Scripture, saying that we don't live by bread alone (Deuteronomy 8:3). This states that we should live on every word that comes from God's mouth. What God says matters more than what we eat.

After Jesus thwarts the devil's first attempt to distract him from his ministry, Satan tries again. He takes Jesus to a lofty vantage point where they can survey all the nations in the entire world. Satan, having control over the world for a time, promises to cede it to Jesus if he will merely bow down and worship him.

Jesus won't. He quotes Scripture again. It says we are to worship and serve only the Lord God (Deuteronomy 6:13).

The devil has now failed twice to tempt Jesus.

But he has another idea. This time he'll quote Scripture to Jesus. The enemy will use the Word of God to try to manipulate him.

From the highest point of the temple, Satan taunts Jesus. He says, "*If* you are the Son of God, jump. Scripture says God will send his angels to protect you and keep you from harm" (Psalm 91:11–12).

Notice that the devil questions Jesus's divinity as God's Son. This begs for Jesus to defend his identity. But he doesn't take the bait. Instead, he responds with a Scripture verse of his own. He says to not test the Lord God (Deuteronomy 6:16).

At this point, Satan retreats from tempting Jesus and waits for a more opportune time.

Questions: *Do we know the Bible well enough to use it to defend ourselves when Satan attacks us? How should we react when the devil throws Scripture at us?*

Prayer: Father God, may we hide your Word in our heart so that we will not sin against you (Psalm 119:11).

DAY 4: FISHING FOR PEOPLE

TODAY'S PASSAGE: MARK 1:14–20, WITH
MATTHEW 4:18–22, LUKE 5:1–11, AND JOHN
1:35–51

Focus verse: *"Come, follow me," Jesus said, "and I will
send you out to fish for people."* (Mark 1:17)

Having been victorious over Satan's attempts to distract Jesus from pursuing his mission—his calling—Jesus invites his first followers. In Mark's concise account of this event, Jesus tells the crowd, "It's time! God's kingdom is within reach. Repent and believe this good news."

After he shares his message, Jesus invites two fishermen, Simon Peter and his brother Andrew, to come and follow him. Jesus will teach them how to fish for people. Abandoning their nets and their boats, the brothers do just that.

Further down the shore, Jesus calls two more fishermen, James and John, to follow him as well. They, too, walk away from their life's work, leaving their father Zebedee, and his hired hands, behind.

In Luke's more detailed account, we see Jesus preaching to a crowd gathered at Lake Gennesaret, also known as the Sea of Galilee. Knowing that sound travels better over water, Jesus gets into Simon Peter's boat and asks him to row out a bit from shore. From this vantage, Jesus preaches to the crowd.

Though Luke doesn't share Jesus's message, Matthew and Mark both give brief summaries of what the teacher says: repent for God's kingdom is near. None of the gospel accounts, however, share the crowd's reaction, but Luke tells us that after Jesus ends his message, he asks Peter to go into deeper waters and cast their nets.

Peter objects, explaining that they fished all night and caught nothing. But for some reason, Peter does what Jesus asks, even though they're tired and the ideal time to fish has passed.

When Peter and Andrew cast their nets into the sea, they catch so many fish that their nets are about to break. Peter and Andrew beckon James and John for help. The large catch threatens to swamp both boats. At this point, Peter drops to his knees at Jesus's feet and proclaims himself to be unworthy to be in Jesus's presence.

Jesus ignores what Peter says and instead tells him not to be afraid. "From now on, you will catch people instead of fish."

Having witnessed a miracle, Peter and his cohorts accept Jesus's challenge and follow him. They abandon their family fishing business and instead start fishing for people for the kingdom of God. It's a higher calling for a greater purpose, and they're quick to follow Jesus.

Though this is the first time Jesus gets the fishermen's attention with a miraculous catch, it won't be the last. After he dies for the wrong things we've done and rises from the dead, some of his followers will experience another miraculous catch of fish. Jesus will get their attention again, this time confirming he's alive. This second extraordinary catch (John 21:1–14) reminds them of his initial call to fish for people.

Questions: *What is Jesus calling us to do to grow his kingdom? Whether miraculous or ordinary, what has Jesus done to get our attention?*

Prayer: Jesus, may we fish for people to bring them to you and grow the kingdom of God.

DAY 5: A WEDDING TO REMEMBER
TODAY'S PASSAGE: JOHN 2:1–11

Focus verse: *What Jesus did here in Cana of Galilee was the first of the signs through which he revealed his glory; and his disciples believed in him.* (John 2:11)

Next, in our narrative of Jesus's life, we'll consider some events from John's account about Jesus's early ministry. We'll start with Jesus's first public miracle, which occurs shortly after his baptism (see Day 2).

Though we'll later see Jesus healing people, casting out evil spirits, and raising the dead, his first miracle is less astounding. It's almost trivial. Yet it's still a miracle: a supernatural occurrence that's physically impossible.

What is this miracle? Jesus makes wine from water at a party.

A few days after Jesus calls his first four disciples —Peter, Andrew, James, and John—they all go to a wedding. It's in Cana, a part of Galilee. Jesus's mother, Mary, is there too.

The groom didn't plan well and runs out of wine. Maybe it was all he could afford to buy. If so, he should have invited fewer people.

Regardless, it's a social disaster, a public embarrassment for him and his bride. It shows disrespect for his guests. They'll grumble about his shortsightedness for the rest of the party instead of celebrating his marriage. And they'll remember his failure at every wedding for years to come.

Yet, on a supernatural level, running out of wine at a wedding threatens no one's well-being. Since many have already drunk too much, they may be better off not drinking any more.

Jesus could use this as a teachable moment to warn against the sin of overconsumption, of becoming drunk (Ephesians 5:18). It would seem a fantastic way to launch his public ministry. But he doesn't do that.

Mary, aware of what happened, edges up to Jesus and whispers, "They ran out of wine."

Jesus dismisses her concern. "It's not my problem," he says. "Besides, it's not my time."

She ignores him and tells the servants, "Do whatever he says." She's done what she can and trusts Jesus to do what she cannot.

Despite telling Mary he doesn't want to get involved, Jesus does anyway. He tells the servants to fill six containers with water. Together, these vessels will hold over one hundred gallons. The servants do as instructed. Jesus tells them, "Take a sample to the master of ceremonies."

The man takes a sip of the water, which Jesus has now miraculously turned into wine. The master of the wedding banquet praises the bridegroom for saving the best wine for last. This contrasts with the typical practice of serving the choice wine first and holding back the lesser vintages for when people have drunk too much to care.

Jesus's disciples are there to witness this miracle. Though the miraculous catch was for them alone, the miraculous wine occurred in a public setting for all to see. In doing so, Jesus further reveals his power to his disciples. And John writes that they believe in him as a result.

Questions*: Do we need to see a miracle or sign before we believe in Jesus? How does knowing that Jesus provided wine at a wedding encourage us to trust him to provide what we need each day?*

Prayer: Jesus, supply what we need today. May we always remember to thank you for your provisions.

DAY 6: CONSUMED WITH ZEAL
TODAY'S PASSAGE: JOHN 2:13–25

Focus verse: *Jesus answered them, "Destroy this temple, and I will raise it again in three days."* (John 2:19)

Shortly after the wedding feast, where Jesus turns water into wine, Jesus travels to Jerusalem for the Passover celebration.

He goes to the temple. In the courtyard, he finds people conducting business instead of worshiping God. The merchants sell sheep, cattle, and doves, which the worshippers need for various rites and sacrifices, as required by the Old Testament law. Though they could bring these animals from their own farms, many travel a long distance over several days to reach the temple, so it's practical for them to leave their animals at home and buy what they need when they arrive.

Other businesspeople serve as a currency exchange. They make a nice profit for their efforts, earning a commission on each transaction.

Both groups enable worship. But they don't belong in the temple courts, at the very doors to the temple.

They show disrespect—contempt even—for the temple. They exploit religious practices to earn a living. Jesus is irate. He makes a whip. "Get out!" he screams as he drives the vendors and their animals out of the temple's courtyard. Aggressively, he throws over the tables of the money changers. Coins scatter. "Get out! My Father's house is not a marketplace!"

No one stops him.

The suppliers flee.

His disciples remember David's psalm, where he proclaims for himself and prophesies about the coming Savior that "zeal for your house consumes me" (Psalm 9:9).

Jesus's actions promote worship that respects his Father and the temple as a place of worship. This event, however, doesn't give us permission to get violent for God. Instead, it reminds us to not let money or worldly activities encroach on our worship space or distract from our worship time, which we should carefully protect as holy.

Though no one stops Jesus from his aggressive expulsion of these sellers from the temple, some people question his authority to act. The Jewish leaders certainly didn't grant him permission. In fact, the merchants are likely there because of the religious leaders' approval. They may even get a percentage of the profits.

So, when asked for a sign to prove his authority, Jesus simply says, "Destroy this temple, and I'll raise it again in three days."

Recalling that it took forty-six years to build the temple, they know it's not possible for Jesus to rebuild it in three days.

Yet when Jesus refers to "this temple," he doesn't mean the physical temple that stands before them but the temple of his body. We'll later read in Scripture that Jesus does what he said. After the Jewish leaders destroy his body through crucifixion, he restores it by rising from the dead.

Questions: *What practices do we do today that might make Jesus angry? How can our worship today revere Father God more fully?*

Prayer: Jesus, may our worship of you be pure and honorable.

DAY 7: YOU MUST BE BORN AGAIN
TODAY'S PASSAGE: JOHN 3:1–21

Focus verse: *Jesus replied, "Very truly I tell you, no one can see the kingdom of God unless they are born again.* (John 3:3)

We only read about Nicodemus in the book of John. Nicodemus comes to Jesus, but he arrives in secret at night, under the shroud of darkness. He's a member of the religious council that opposes Jesus.

If they discover Nicodemus is interested in Jesus, it will ruin his standing in the religious community. He fears his associates will expel him from the council and Jewish society will ostracize him. It's a risk he's not willing to take. That's why he meets Jesus at night.

He has questions, and his religious training doesn't provide answers.

He finds Jesus and shows respect by calling him Rabbi, which means *teacher*. But before Nicodemus can ask his question, Jesus gives the answer. "To be part of God's kingdom, you must be born again."

This confuses Nicodemus. "What? How can an adult be reborn as a baby?"

Jesus explains. "There's physical birth, being born of water. And there's spiritual birth, being born through the Holy Spirit. That's what it means to be born again."

Nicodemus is still confused. "How so?"

"Once I sacrifice myself, everyone who believes in me and what I've done will have eternal life," Jesus says.

He restates the importance of belief in the best-known verse in the Bible, John 3:16, which says if we believe in Jesus, we'll have eternal life. The next verse adds that Jesus comes to save us, not to condemn us—that is, he doesn't judge us.

Jesus continues his explanation. "Everyone who believes faces no condemnation. But those who don't believe stand condemned already."

To be born again means to believe in Jesus. To emphasize belief as the essential requirement—and to make sure we don't miss it—Jesus repeats it three times (verses 15, 16, and 18).

The Bible doesn't record Nicodemus's response to Jesus's call to be born again by believing in him. But we can infer that he does. Though Nicodemus first approaches Jesus in private, he will later take a public stand to defend Jesus and after that to help bury his body (John 7:50–51 and John 19:38–42).

Nicodemus's actions show he is born again.

Questions: *To be born again, all you need to do is believe in Jesus. Will you do that now? And if you're already born again, do your actions prove that you follow Jesus?*

Prayer: Thank you, Jesus, for coming to earth to save us and give us eternal life.

DAY 8: DRINK LIVING WATER

TODAY'S PASSAGE: JOHN 4:1–42

Focus verse: *Jesus answered, "Everyone who drinks this water will be thirsty again, but whoever drinks the water I give them will never thirst. Indeed, the water I give them will become in them a spring of water welling up to eternal life."*
(John 4:13–14)

In Jesus's day, few people had access to running water. They went to a well every day to draw the water they'd need. We see this in today's passage.

Jesus and his disciples head to Galilee. Instead of traveling around Samaria, as was the customary practice among Jews, they take a direct path and walk straight through the region. Along the way, they stop in Sychar.

Jesus sends his disciples into town to buy food, while he rests at the town well. It's midday.

A woman comes to fetch water. Everyone else would've gotten their daily supply in the early morning when it's cooler. We assume she goes at noon because during the heat of the day, no one else will be there. She has a sordid past and an unacceptable present. She wants to lessen her inter-actions with others, protecting herself from their glares and judgment.

When she arrives, she sees a man waiting by the well. This is unexpected. He talks to her. This is even more startling. The man asks her for a drink. This surprises her because it's unacceptable.

The first problem is a Jewish man talking to a Samaritan woman. The second issue is that Jesus will need to drink from her cup. Religious Jews would seek to avoid both.

Now he shocks her even more. "If you knew who I was, you'd ask me for living water."

Jesus's words to her have a parallel theme to what he told Nicodemus in yesterday's reading about being born again. There is a physical birth and a subsequent spiritual birth, of being born again. In the same way, there is tangible water to quench our physical thirst and supernatural water to quench our spiritual yearning. Jesus offers us this living water.

When Jesus mentions living water, she assumes he means the physical water in the well, but he's referring to spiritual water. It's the kind that supplies eternal life.

To prove his supernatural power to give her this never-be-thirsty-again living water, Jesus reveals he knows about her situation. He knows everything: her five marriages and her present living arrangement.

But Jesus accepts her despite the lifestyle she leads. He offers her love even though she doesn't deserve it. He doesn't criticize her life choices. In this way, Jesus shows her grace and mercy. He doesn't judge her. Instead, he accepts her for who she is.

Leaving her water jar behind, she scurries back to town to tell everyone what Jesus said. They're intrigued. Based on her testimony, they come out to meet him and see for themselves. They believe in him and beg him to stay. His journey can wait. He spends two more days with them before resuming his trip to Galilee.

The woman seeks water to temporarily satisfy her body. But Jesus offers her living water to permanently save her spirit. She only needs to believe in him to receive it.

Questions: *Have we followed the example of the Samaritan woman and told others about Jesus and the living water he offers? Is our testimony convincing enough that others might believe?*

Prayer: Jesus, may we drink your living water and never thirst again.

DAY 9: SCRIPTURE FULFILLED

TODAY'S PASSAGE: LUKE 4:16–30

Focus verse: *"Today this scripture is fulfilled in your hearing."* (Luke 4:21)

I n the region of Galilee, Jesus returns to his hometown, Nazareth. He goes to the synagogue on the Sabbath. The people gather, and he reads from the book of Isaiah (Isaiah 61:1–2).

The passage contains a future-focused foretelling of the coming Messiah. Reading from this prophecy, Jesus proclaims that God's Spirit is in him, anointing him to:

- tell God's good news to poor people,

- decree freedom to the prisoners,
- heal the blind,
- free the oppressed, and
- proclaim God's favor.

After reading this passage, Jesus sits. Everyone watches.

With their attention fixed on him, he says, "This text is about me and what I'm here to do." They're amazed at his words and speak highly of him.

If only Jesus would stop at this point, but he doesn't.

Instead, he launches into a sermon. He's blunt. "People never accept a hometown prophet." He reminds them of two stories from Scripture.

The first one is about the prophet Elijah (1 Kings 17:7–16). During a three-year drought, he leaves the country of Israel and travels to Zarephath, in Sidon. There he meets a struggling widow. She's preparing the last meal for her and her son before they starve to death.

Miraculously, God multiplies her meager supply of flour and oil to feed her, her son, and Elijah throughout the drought. Though there are many needy widows in Israel, God sent Elijah to help a foreigner.

Next is Naaman (2 Kings 5:1–14). He's the commander of the Syrian army that has oppressed the nation of Israel. But Naaman has leprosy. The prophet Elisha heals him, even though many people in the nation of Israel also have leprosy. Not only does God heal a foreigner, but this foreigner has oppressed God's people.

These examples show God favoring outsiders instead of his chosen people.

Though everything Jesus says is true, the people don't care. They're insulted. They rage at him for mentioning these two stories. A mob forms. They drive Jesus out of town, planning to throw him off a cliff to kill him.

But it's not his time. Jesus simply walks through the crowd and leaves unscathed.

Questions: *When we hear words that offend us, do we attack the messenger even if it's true? Will we speak God's truth even if it's unpopular?*

Prayer: Heavenly Father, may we boldly proclaim your truth to others, regardless of the cost.

DAY 10: JESUS'S AUTHORITY

TODAY'S PASSAGE: MARK 1:21–34, WITH MATTHEW 8:14–17 AND LUKE 4:31–41

Focus verse: *The people were all so amazed that they asked each other, "What is this? A new teaching—and with authority! He even gives orders to impure spirits and they obey him."* (Mark 1:27)

On another Sabbath, Jesus and his disciples are in Capernaum. Once again, he goes to the synagogue to address the people who gather. His teaching amazes them. He speaks with authority, which is quite unlike the teachers of the law the Jews usually hear.

We can understand this reference to authority as Jesus's approach to teaching. He doesn't quote other teachers or repeat what they say. Jesus has the power—he has the right—to say what he says. This is authority. His words carry a freshness that gets the people's attention and draws them to him.

At this point a man with an impure spirit cries out to Jesus. "What do you want with us? Will you destroy us? I know you're God's Holy One!"

Jesus doesn't answer the man. Instead, he tells him to be quiet. Next, he commands the spirit to leave. The spirit obeys, giving a departing shriek in protest.

Though we can debate the meaning of an impure spirit, we can agree that the man is better now that the impure spirit has left. Jesus improved the man's life. That's what our Savior does.

The people are even more impressed.

Jesus backed up his words with action. This proves his authority, his power, to say the things he does. Again, they marvel at his new teaching, one with integrity. By casting out the impure spirit, Jesus confirms his power.

This reminds us of what James will later write when he says that it's much easier to prove our faith by what we do, instead of with words only (James 2:14–26). So too with Jesus's teaching then—and our teaching today.

Jesus and his followers leave the synagogue and

head to Peter and Andrew's home. Peter's mother-in-law is down with a high fever. They tell Jesus. He goes to her and helps her get up. When she stands, the fever leaves. She's back to normal.

That night the people flock to Jesus. They bring all who are sick or possessed by demons. He heals them and drives out their tormentors.

In doing so, Jesus continues to prove his authority. He will later impart that authority to his disciples (Matthew 28:18–20) and by extension to us today.

Questions: *How can we better teach others with authority, like Jesus? How can we help others in Jesus's name?*

Prayer: Jesus, may we speak with authority and heal with authority, just like you.

DAY 11: JESUS HEALS AND SAVES

TODAY'S PASSAGE: MARK 2:1–12, WITH
MATTHEW 9:1–8 AND LUKE 5:17–26

Focus verse: *"Which is easier: to say to this paralyzed man, 'Your sins are forgiven,' or to say, 'Get up, take your mat and walk'?"* (Mark 2:9)

After Jesus heals many people, Mark shares another healing that happens a few days later. It is both specific and spectacular.

Some men come carrying a paralyzed man. They've heard about Jesus and his healing power. They have confidence he can heal their friend. Yet when they arrive at the house where Jesus is speaking, the place is packed. They can't reach him.

Though the practical thing to do would be to

wait outside for Jesus to leave, they don't want to. They feel an urgency in their quest. They go up to the rooftop of the home and dig through it. This implies they make a hole in the roof, something the homeowner wouldn't be pleased about. In Luke's account, however, he says they remove some tiles. I prefer this nondestructive explanation.

Regardless, their task would be neither quick nor quiet. Their effort to access Jesus would disturb his teaching and distract the people gathered to listen. Once they open the roof, they lower the paralyzed man right in front of Jesus.

Jesus addresses the man's most pressing need, though it's not what the people perceive he needs most.

Jesus tells the man, "Your sins are forgiven."

The religious leaders are aghast at his audacity. *Who does this Jesus think he is?* they wonder. *It's blasphemous. Only God can forgive sins.*

Jesus knows their thoughts. He challenges their judgmental attitudes. "Which is easier," he asks, "to forgive sins or heal a paralyzed man?"

To prove he has the power to forgive sins, Jesus heals the man by telling him to get up, take his mat, and go home. To the crowd's delight, the man does.

Jesus first addressed the man's greatest need, by

forgiving his sins. Then he addressed the man's second greatest need by healing him and restoring his ability to walk.

In this story we get insight into Jesus's mission. He came to heal *and* to save.

At that time, the people accepted Jesus's healing ministry, but not so much his saving ministry.

Today, it's the opposite. His followers accept his saving ministry, but not so much his healing ministry.

This wonderful story covers both.

Jesus heals the man to prove he has the authority to forgive sins.

Yes, Jesus came to heal and to save. He did it then, and he does it today. All we need to do is believe and receive.

Questions: *How well do we do at recognizing Jesus as our Savior* and *as our Healer? What must we do to better celebrate him as accomplishing both?*

Prayer: Jesus, we praise you for your saving power and your healing power.

DAY 12: PICKING GRAIN ON THE SABBATH

TODAY'S PASSAGE: MARK 2:23–28, WITH
MATTHEW 12:1–8 AND LUKE 6:1–5

Focus verse: *Then [Jesus] said to them, "The Sabbath was made for man, not man for the Sabbath."* (Mark 2:27)

One day, Jesus and his disciples walk through a field of grain. It's the Sabbath. They're hungry. They pick some of the heads of grain and eat them. I doubt the disciples would have done this on their own, so likely Jesus does it first, and they follow his example.

Jesus's detractors—the Pharisees—see what's happening. They're quick to criticize him. They judge that picking grain to eat is akin to harvesting. Harvesting grain on the Sabbath is prohibited because it constitutes work. Their law tells them to rest on the Sabbath and not do any labor.

Therefore, Jesus and his disciples have shown a blatant disregard for the Old Testament law. And the religious leaders are quick to point this out.

Jesus clarifies their thinking by recalling another Scripture passage. He reminds them of David fleeing from King Saul. David was hungry and asked the priest for food. The only thing available was the consecrated bread, which only the priests could eat, not David, and not his men. Yet the priest determined it was okay to make an exception. He gave David the consecrated bread.

If this was okay and didn't result in any punishment, implicitly, it's permissible to work on the Sabbath when you're hungry and need to eat.

Matthew adds that Jesus reminds the Pharisees about the priests who work on the Sabbath while doing their tasks, as assigned by God. Yet they're innocent of breaking the law to rest and not do any work on the last day of the week.

God set the example for this way back in the book of Genesis—centuries before giving Moses the command to rest on the Sabbath and keep it holy (Deuteronomy 5:14). After God created us, our world, and our reality in six days, he rested on the seventh (Genesis 2:2–3).

Jesus gives us some perspective on this. He says the Sabbath—that is, the prescribed day of rest—was made for man and not man for the Sabbath. By our convention today, most followers of Jesus view Sunday as their Sabbath. Therefore, we can paraphrase Jesus's words to say that Sunday is made for us, not us for Sunday.

We'll do well to consider Jesus's teaching and example so we can best apply it to our lives today.

Questions: *How should we treat the Sabbath? How can we find a balance between doing nothing—with legalistic fervor—and working like we would on any other day?*

Prayer: Jesus, we acknowledge you as Lord, even of the Sabbath.

DAY 13: JESUS HEALS ON THE SABBATH

TODAY'S PASSAGE: MARK 3:1–6, WITH
MATTHEW 12:9–14 AND LUKE 6:6–11

Focus verse: *Then Jesus asked them, "Which is lawful on the Sabbath: to do good or to do evil, to save life or to kill?"* (Mark 3:4)

N ext, Mark shares a related story. Later that day—after picking grain on the Sabbath and eating it—Jesus goes to the synagogue. There's a man with a shriveled hand.

The Pharisees watch Jesus with intention to see what he'll do. Though they failed in their attempt to accuse him of working on the Sabbath, they sense that another opportunity to confront him is about to present itself.

Though Mark doesn't mention it, Matthew says

Jesus asks the people, "Is it legal to heal on the Sabbath day?" They don't respond. Luke, however, explains that Jesus already knows what they're thinking.

Regardless, Jesus calls the man forward and has him stand before the people. Having captured everyone's attention, Jesus has a teachable moment.

"Which is better," he asks, "to do good on the Sabbath or to cause harm? To save a life or destroy it?"

Matthew records a different part of Jesus's lesson. "Which of you," Jesus asks, "would rescue your sheep that fell into a pit on the Sabbath?" Since a person is much more precious than any animal, it's certainly legal to do good things for others on the Sabbath.

Jesus tells the man to stretch out his hand. As he does, his hand becomes completely restored. He is made whole.

Though Jesus neither proclaims healing on the man nor places his hand on the man to impart healing, no one doubts that Jesus healed him.

Rather than celebrate a man whose body has been restored to full functionality, the Pharisees—still placing their legalistic ideals above doing good for others—stomp off. They plot how they might kill Jesus. They're too focused on their religious practices to see that Jesus provides them with a better way to celebrate God on the Sabbath.

May we seek ways to be more like Jesus and less like the Pharisees when it comes to our Sunday observances.

Questions*: Which of our practices or attitudes must we change to better apply Jesus's teaching to do good? When have we clung to rules and missed opportunities to help others?*

Prayer: Jesus, give us eyes to see opportunities to do good—to save a life—that you place before us each day, and especially on Sunday.

DAY 14: A FIRM FOUNDATION
TODAY'S PASSAGE: MATTHEW 7:21–29

Focus verse: *"Therefore everyone who hears these words of mine and puts them into practice is like a wise man who built his house on the rock."* (Matthew 7:24)

We find Jesus's longest and best-known sermon in Matthew 5–7. We often call it the Sermon on the Mount. In it, Jesus covers an array of countercultural ideas about what it means to truly follow him. Not only are his words countercultural, but they're also counter-religious. That is, they're contrary to the prevailing religious thinking of his audience—both then and even today.

Therefore, it's not surprising that when Jesus

finishes speaking, Matthew notes that the crowds were amazed with his teaching. He spoke with authority and not like the teachers of the law (Matthew 7:28–29). We also covered his authority in Day 10.

One of Jesus's concluding thoughts in the Sermon on the Mount is our focus verse for today. He says that anyone who hears his words *and* obeys them is like a wise person who builds his house on a rock-solid footing. Yes, Jesus's words—as recorded in the Bible—are the foundation for our faith.

If we don't remain anchored in Scripture—and especially in Jesus's words—our faith becomes untethered from its biblical base. Without this foundation, we risk disconnecting our beliefs and practices from what Jesus prescribes and wants.

Therefore, it's critical that we cling to the words of the Bible and especially the words of Jesus. Though Jesus's words primarily appear in the Bible's four biographies about him—Matthew, Mark, Luke, and John—they also occur in four other books in the New Testament: Acts, 1 Corinthians, 2 Corinthians, and especially Revelation. We'll do well to consider these passages also.

To focus our attention on what Jesus says, we

can go through the above eight books with a high-lighter to emphasize them. Or we can use a version of the Bible that shows Jesus's words in red, a red-letter edition.

As we covered in Day 3, we should hide God's Word in our hearts (Psalm 119:11). And the Sermon on the Mount is an ideal place to start. We could spend years—even a lifetime—mining its many truths. Why not start today?

Questions*: How can we better know Jesus's words and apply them to our lives each day? What are some of Jesus's teachings that we know but haven't yet obeyed?*

Prayer: Thank you, Jesus, for your words as recorded in the Bible. May we read them and do what you tell us to do.

DAY 15: THE FAITH OF THE CENTURION

TODAY'S PASSAGE: MATTHEW 8:5–13 AND LUKE 7:1–10

Focus verse: *When Jesus heard this, he was amazed at [the centurion], and turning to the crowd following him, he said, "I tell you, I have not found such great faith even in Israel."* (Luke 7:9)

In Capernaum is a centurion, a commander in the Roman army who has one hundred soldiers under his authority. He has a valued servant who is sick and about to die. Matthew adds that the servant is paralyzed and in great pain.

It's not even one of the centurion's soldiers who needs help, but his servant. In Luke's version, this centurion heard about Jesus and sends some Jewish elders to ask Jesus to come and heal the man.

Oh, how this must pain the elders. They oppose Jesus and view him as a threat to their religion and way of life. Yet they dare not tell the centurion no. Instead, they condescend themselves to ask Jesus for a favor.

Citing the centurion's worthiness, they tell Jesus that he loves their nation and even built their synagogue. This seems highly unusual, yet it shows he's positively predisposed toward them and their beliefs, even though he's an outsider and not accepted. Not only is he a Gentile, but he's also part of the Roman occupying force that oppresses them.

Once the Jewish elders make their request to Jesus, he heads with them to the centurion's home. It's important to remember that, as a Jew, Jesus shouldn't enter the house of a non-Jew, a Gentile (John 18:28 and Acts 10:28). But this doesn't seem to be an issue for him. And it shouldn't be for us.

Though Jesus has already healed others, they've all been Jews, his own people. Will he also heal a non-Jew? He intends to.

But before he arrives, the centurion sends a message to Jesus. "Don't trouble yourself to come to my home. I don't deserve to have you enter my house. Just proclaim healing and my servant will be made well."

Citing his authority over his soldiers and their obedience to his commands, the centurion acknowledges Jesus's authority and a belief that illness is likewise subject to Jesus's command.

The centurion's faith amazes Jesus. He proclaims it as the greatest faith he has seen, surpassing his own people, even his followers and disciples.

When the messengers return to the centurion's home, they find the servant is better. Jesus healed him.

Questions: *Do we have faith that Jesus can heal today? Would our friends say that we have a deep faith or a shallow one?*

Prayer: Father God, may we have a faith like the centurion. May our confidence in you be an encouragement to others.

DAY 16: JESUS RAISES THE WIDOW'S SON

TODAY'S PASSAGE: LUKE 7:11–17

Focus verse: *When the Lord saw her, his heart went out to her and he said, "Don't cry." (Luke 7:13)*

S hortly after healing the centurion's servant in Capernaum, Jesus heads to the town of Nain. Interestingly, this is the only time we find Nain mentioned in the Bible. It must be a small, remote, or unworthy place. Yet Jesus goes there anyway. Small, remote, and unworthy isn't an issue for him. We can learn from his example.

With his disciples in tow and followed by a large crowd, Jesus approaches the city. He encounters a funeral procession. It's for a young man, the only son of a widow.

In that day, a woman with neither husband nor son would find it hard to eke out a living. Her son's death would signal the end of her existence as she knew it. Poverty would mark her life, and constant struggles would comprise her remaining days. Her future looks bleak.

Many people from Nain are with her as part of the funeral procession.

When Jesus sees her, he understands her predicament. He feels compassion for her from the depths of his heart. He tells her not to cry. Approaching the litter that carries the young man's body, Jesus touches it.

We can imagine a collective gasp coming from the people in the funeral procession, as well as the people following Jesus. In effect, he touched a dead person. Jewish law prohibits contact with a dead body, for it would make them unclean, that is, defiled (see Leviticus 22:4, as well as Haggai 2:13).

Yet being labeled unclean or defiled doesn't matter to Jesus. What matters is the woman's sorrow and her future.

When he touches the funeral bier, the pall-bearers stop. Jesus commands the young man—the corpse—to get up. The dead man, now very much alive, sits up and starts talking. Jesus gives him back to his mother. His life is restored, along with her future.

Though Jesus has already performed many miracles and healed multiple people, this is the first person he's raised from the dead. It shows his resurrection power and hints at what will happen after his execution.

Questions: *How willing are we to set societal or religious conventions aside to help those in need? Do our actions show we care more about what people think or about what God thinks?*

Prayer: Jesus, may we follow your example to help others every time we can, regardless of the circumstances.

DAY 17: ANOINTED FOR MINISTRY
TODAY'S PASSAGE: LUKE 7:36–50

Focus verse: *"Your faith has saved you; go in peace."*
(Luke 7:50)

Each of the gospel accounts of Jesus's life give a story of a woman who anoints Jesus. Besides today's text in Luke, we have Matthew 26:6–13, Mark 14:3–9, and John 12:1–8.

Most people assume these refer to the same event, even though some details differ or conflict. But there could have been multiple anointings. For example, Matthew and Mark say the woman anoints Jesus's head. This symbolically prepares him for burial. Luke, however, says the woman anoints

Jesus's feet. This symbolically prepares him for ministry.

Since we are early in Jesus's ministry at this point in our timeline, we'll cover Luke's version.

Simon, a Pharisee, invites Jesus over for dinner.

Pharisees are religious insiders. They follow the law of Moses with zeal and adhere to thousands of other rules they made up over the years to guide them in the right way to live. To their credit, they are righteous, but they're also legalistic. Today's most religious person wouldn't come close to matching the Pharisees' rigid lifestyle.

Though Jesus loves everyone, he often criticizes Pharisees. They miss the point of what God intends. Jesus wants to correct their perspective, but they oppose him.

Given this, it's unlikely a Pharisee would seek Jesus and want to eat with him. But that's exactly what this Pharisee does.

Yet when Jesus shows up, Simon doesn't offer him the socially appropriate welcome: wash his feet, greet him with a kiss, or anoint his head.

Jesus, Simon, and the rest of his guests recline at Simon's table. Contrary to how this is often portrayed, they don't sit *around* a table. Instead, they lie on their sides, leaning on their elbows, with their heads toward a low table and their legs pointing out.

A woman with a sinful lifestyle comes to Jesus. Before we harshly judge her, remember, we have all sinned (Romans 3:23).

She arrives ready to show how much she loves Jesus. This might be her only chance. She stands behind his feet as he reclines at the table. Overcome with emotion, she weeps. Her tears fall on his feet. Without a towel to dry them, she uses her hair. She kisses his feet and pours her perfume over them. She empties the bottle. The aroma fills the room.

In his mind, Simon criticizes the woman for her inappropriate lifestyle and Jesus for allowing a sinful woman to touch him.

Jesus knows Simon's thoughts. The teacher shares a story about forgiveness. He recounts how Simon neglected to wash and dry Jesus's feet, greet him with a kiss, and put oil on him. But this woman did all three.

Jesus tells the woman, "Your sins are forgiven." While the guests murmur their disapproval, Jesus adds, "Because of your faith, you are saved."

The woman's path to salvation is simple: worship Jesus and love him.

Questions: *Is worshiping Jesus and loving him enough for us to be saved? How often do we judge others, like Simon judged both the woman and Jesus?*

Prayer: Jesus, show us the right way to worship and love you.

DAY 18: A BUMPER CROP

TODAY'S PASSAGE: MARK 4:1–20, WITH MATTHEW 13:1–23 AND LUKE 8:4–15

Focus verse: *"Others, like seed sown on good soil, hear the word, accept it, and produce a crop—some thirty, some sixty, some a hundred times what was sown."* (Mark 4:20)

Matthew, Mark, and Luke, record the parables of Jesus. Collectively, there are forty of them in the Bible. A parable is a story from the real world that reveals spiritual truth.

Though the references to Jesus's parables were easy for his audience to understand two thousand years ago, they may not be as accessible to us today. Nonetheless, Jesus's parables remain worthy of our consideration.

Today we'll cover one of them, along with Jesus's explanation. In this way, we can use his teaching about this parable as a model to help us better understand the others.

This parable is of a man planting seed. He does this by scattering it with his hand in the area where it needs to go. This is imprecise, however, with not all the seed ending up in the ideal location.

Some seeds end up on the path. The birds quickly eat them. Other seeds fall among the rocks where there's little soil. These seeds sprout quickly, but they die because they lack good roots. A third scenario is seeds that fall among weeds. Though it grows, the weeds crowd it, and it cannot produce. But the seeds that fall on the good soil grows and produces a crop, with a yield of thirty, sixty, or even a hundredfold.

When the disciples ask Jesus to explain the parable, he gives them a concise answer.

The farmer—whom we implicitly know is Jesus —sows seed. The seed is the word, the good news about salvation. The four places the seed falls reveal four responses to Jesus's message.

Birds that eat the seed on the path symbolize Satan, who is quick to remove Jesus's message from people's minds. The seed that sprouts in rocky places represents people whose faith has no roots and doesn't last. It soon withers and dies. And the seed that falls among the weeds and is choked out characterizes people who allow wealth and worldly pursuits to distract them from following Jesus. They produce no fruit.

Yet the seed that falls on the good soil exemplifies people who hear the good news of Jesus and follow him. Then they tell others, who also follow him. They bring thirty, sixty, or even one hundred more people into the kingdom of God.

Questions: *Which types of soil in this parable best represent our lives? What are we doing to produce a crop—a bumper crop—for Jesus?*

Prayer: Heavenly Father, may we tell others about Jesus and help grow your kingdom.

DAY 19: AUTHORITY OVER CREATION

TODAY'S PASSAGE: MARK 4:35–41, WITH MATTHEW 8:23–27 AND LUKE 8:22–25

Focus verse: *[Jesus] got up, rebuked the wind and said to the waves, "Quiet! Be still!" Then the wind died down and it was completely calm.* (Mark 4:39)

That evening—after Jesus gave his parable of the farmer planting his seeds, along with several other teachings—he suggests his disciples go to the other side of the lake. This likely refers to the Sea of Galilee.

As they do, they leave the crowd behind. This seems counterintuitive, an unwise move. Jesus had spoken to a group of people, but instead of building on the foundation he's established, he leaves. This doesn't seem like any way to grow a ministry. Yet that's what Jesus does.

Since Jesus is both God and human, his human side is tired after preaching all day. Yes, public speaking is draining. And Jesus needs rest. He finds a comfortable cushion on the boat.

In the open water, a squall develops. It grows into a furious storm. Waves break over the side of the vessel and threaten to sink it. Yet Jesus is unaware of what's happening around him. He's sleeping in the back of the boat.

In a panic, his disciples wake him. "Don't you care that we're about to drown?"

Jesus—whom I suspect is peeved to have his rest interrupted—gets up. He chides the wind; he reprimands the waves. "Quiet!" he calls out. "Be still!"

The winds cease to blow, and the waves calm.

Jesus turns his attention to his disciples. "Why are you wallowing in fear? Where is your faith?" At this point, I envision the irritated Jesus returning to his cushion in the back of the boat to finish his nap.

We're left to wonder if the faith Jesus refers to is faith *in* him or faith that the disciples could have controlled the storm *through* him.

For the disciples' part, they're terrified over what they witnessed. They almost drowned in a raging storm, yet Jesus commanded it to stop, and it did. "Who is this man?" they ask. "Even the weather is subject to his authority."

In doing this, Jesus goes beyond demonstrating that he has power over the afflictions in people's bodies, and of life itself, to prove his mastery over the environment. Yet it is his creation. If he made it, why wouldn't it be subject to his command?

What Jesus did shouldn't have surprised the disciples, but it did. And we shouldn't be surprised either, but too many of us are.

Questions: *What can we learn from Jesus commanding the storm to stop? When faced with a crisis of our own, what role does our faith play?*

Prayer: Jesus, we praise you for your creation and acknowledge your authority over it. May we truly worship you through it and because of it.

DAY 20: JESUS HEALS THE DEMON-POSSESSED MAN

TODAY'S PASSAGE: MARK 5:1–20, WITH MATTHEW 8:28–34 AND LUKE 8:26–39

Focus verse: *The people began to plead with Jesus to leave their region.* (Mark 5:17)

After Jesus and his disciples cross the lake, a man approaches him. Luke says the man is naked. What a shocking sight this must have been. Even worse, he's controlled by an impure spirit. But we'll later learn that it's not a single evil spirit in him, but many of them, perhaps a legion.

As followers of Jesus, we have the Holy Spirit living in us. This man does not. He has a host of evil spirits living in him. They torment him. Chains cannot contain him. No one can control him. He

PETER DEHAAN

lives among the tombs—among the dead—an anathema for Jewish people. Yet this man—under the control of evil— lives in this abhorrent place. He would cry out in agony. He would cut himself with stones.

The man runs up to Jesus and falls before him. He screams. "What do you want with me, Jesus? I beg you not to torture me!"

He says this because Jesus had commanded the impure spirit to leave him. But instead of immediately obeying Jesus's command, the demon tries to negotiate.

This is when we learn that the man goes by Legion, because of the many demons in him. Legion begs Jesus not to send them into the Abyss (Luke 8:31). Instead, they prefer a herd of pigs. Jesus agrees.

But when Legion enters the pigs, the animals rush down the hill and throw themselves into the lake. They drown. Since it's unlikely Legion would want to kill the bodies they were now inhabiting, a better understanding is that the pigs killed themselves before Legion could dominate them.

Freed from the controlling demons, the man's sanity returns. Through Jesus, he's made right.

When the herdsmen tell the people in the area

what happened, they come to investigate it for themselves. Though they could revere Jesus for what he did in restoring the formerly demon-possessed man, they do not. Instead, they react in fear. They beg Jesus to leave the area. They don't want him around. All they can see is the dead pigs and the economic loss their deaths represent. They blame Jesus.

The man formerly called Legion, however, sees Jesus differently. He wants to go with the man who healed him and restored him to his right mind. But Jesus says no. Instead, he tells the man to go home and let everyone know what happened.

The man does, and the people are amazed at what Jesus did.

Questions: *How do we react when we encounter supernatural acts we don't understand? How often do we blame God for things that aren't his fault?*

Prayer: Father, Son, and Holy Spirit, may we rightly revere you for who you are and what you do in our lives and the lives of those around us.

DAY 21: WAKE THE DEAD

TODAY'S PASSAGE: MARK 5:21–43, WITH
MATTHEW 9:18–26 AND LUKE 8:40–56

Focus verse: *[Jesus] went in and said to them, "Why all this commotion and wailing? The child is not dead but asleep."* (Mark 5:39)

Today's passage is a delightful one that intertwines two stories, with the second one occurring in the middle of the first.

Though we often view the religious leaders of the day as opposing Jesus, not all of them do. One supporter may have been Simon, the Pharisee we encountered in Day 17. Another is Jairus, whom we'll read about today. He's the town's synagogue leader and, therefore, a prominent Jewish figure in the area. Yet he recognizes Jesus for his healing power.

He comes to Jesus in desperation because his twelve-year-old daughter is dying. Yet he has faith that Jesus can place his hands on her and heal her. Jesus agrees to do what Jairus asks.

As he heads to Jairus's house, an enormous crowd follows, pressing in on all sides. In the throng is a woman who'd been bleeding for twelve years. Though she'd spent all she had on medical care, the doctors only made her condition worse.

Aside from needing to deal physically with continuous bleeding, the presence of blood made her spiritually unclean. This restricted what she could do in society and at the temple.

Yet she believes that if she merely touches Jesus's cloak, his healing power will stream from him and stop her flow of blood. He is her last hope.

She touches his garment and receives immediate relief. Jesus feels healing power leave him. "Who touched me?" The woman comes forward to admit what happened. "Go in peace," he says. "You're healed through your faith."

Though one woman is restored, this delay is costly for Jairus. While stopping for the bleeding woman, news arrives that Jairus's daughter has died. If only Jesus had been more intentional about getting to Jairus's house faster.

But Jesus isn't concerned. He simply tells Jairus, "Don't worry. Just believe."

When Jesus arrives at the synagogue leader's home, a wake has already begun. Jesus rebukes the mourners for their commotion and wailing. "The girl isn't dead! She's merely sleeping."

They laugh at him. They know she's dead.

Taking only Peter, James, John, and the girl's parents, Jesus goes to where she lies. He commands her dead body to get up.

It does.

Though Jesus doesn't arrive in time to heal her, he wasn't too late. He woke her from the dead.

Though we may view the description of someone having fallen asleep as a nice euphemism for having died, Jesus views things differently. To him, raising someone from the dead is no more difficult than us waking someone from their sleep.

In Day 49 we'll read a similar account, when Jesus "wakes" his friend Lazarus by raising him from the dead too (John 11:11–13).

Questions: *Do we recognize Jesus for his healing power today? How does our faith compare to that of the bleeding woman and of Jairus?*

Prayer: Jesus, thank you for saving us *and* healing us.

DAY 22: OFFENDED

TODAY'S PASSAGE: MARK 6:1–6 AND
MATTHEW 13:53–58

Focus verse: *"Isn't this the carpenter? Isn't this Mary's son and the brother of James, Joseph, Judas and Simon? Aren't his sisters here with us?" And they took offense at him.*
(Mark 6:3)

After freeing the demon-possessed man from his torment, healing the bleeding woman from her affliction, and raising Jairus's daughter from the dead, Jesus heads to his hometown.

When I think of going home, I think of going to a comfortable environment and a safe place, a place where I'm loved and accepted. I hope this is what going home means to you as well. But it doesn't work out this way for Jesus.

It's the Sabbath. He goes to the synagogue in his hometown. There he instructs the people gathered. His teaching amazes them . . . and perplexes them.

Many of the people there have known him all his life. He grew up with them. They remember him as a child, what he did as a teenager, and his occupation as an adult—a carpenter. At some point, he may have made something for them using his woodworking skills. They know he didn't receive advanced training about their Scriptures. As a result, they don't view him as a teacher.

They recognize Jesus as a tradesman, like his earthly father, Joseph. His mother still lives there. So do his four brothers and his sisters. Teaching them about the Scriptures is completely out of character for the Jesus they know. They take offense.

Jesus tells them, "A prophet is without honor in his hometown, among his friends and relatives." This reminds us of the adage that familiarity breeds contempt.

Because of their disrespect for him, Mark says he *could not* perform miracles there except lay hands on a few sick people and heal them. Matthew, however, says that because of their lack of faith, Jesus *chose* to only heal a few people. Either way, we see faith as a critical component to receive healing.

And their lack of faith shocks him.

While Jesus applauded the centurion's great faith (see Day 15), he was amazed at the lack of faith among the people in his hometown.

Yet it isn't only his hometown that dismisses him. Many of the Jews—his own people—dismiss him and have a lack of faith too.

Questions: *When has a familiarity that breeds contempt kept us from seeing God at work? When have we let someone's perception of us define us?*

Prayer: Heavenly Father, protect us from what other people think about us and instead strengthen us to do what you call us to do.

DAY 23: HEAL AND TEACH

TODAY'S PASSAGE: MARK 6:7–13, WITH
MATTHEW 10:1–42 AND LUKE 9:1–6

Focus verse: *[Jesus] sent them out to proclaim the kingdom of God and to heal the sick.* (Luke 9:2)

Jesus travels from town to town telling people the good news, but this task doesn't solely rest on him. After modeling how to do ministry, he commissions his twelve disciples to go out on their own.

Matthew, Mark, and Luke all share this event in their biographies of Jesus. Mark's account is the most concise—as is usually the case—and Luke's is similar. Matthew's version is the longest.

They all say that Jesus sends out the twelve disciples, but only Mark says he sends them out two by two. Matthew, however, presents the list of twelve disciples in pairs, implying six teams of two each.

From these three gospel accounts, Jesus authorizes his disciples for their mission. He gives them power and authority to drive out demons and cure diseases and sicknesses.

We've talked about Jesus's authority on Days 6, 10, 11, 14, 15, and 19. In these readings, we see that Jesus has authority, and that he shows his authority. Now he gives his authority to his disciples. And he'll do it again when he commissions them to continue his work after he returns to heaven (Matthew 28:18–20).

As they drive out demons and heal the sick, they also preach a message of repentance. The writers confirm that the disciples do as Jesus instructed, but we don't know the response they receive or the outcome of their work.

From this we get an important principle. When Jesus calls us to do something, our responsibility is to obey. We may realize a huge response, a small response, or no response as we work for our Lord. Regardless, we need to do our part and trust him with the outcome.

Building on what the twelve did, Jesus will later

send out seventy-two to expand their reach even more (Luke 10:1–24). We'll cover this in Day 32.

When Jesus sends his disciples out, they are to heal people and tell them the good news of salvation through him. Today we focus on the message part and overlook the healing part.

Yet Jesus came to earth to heal *and* to save. We should do the same.

Questions: *How does Jesus give us his power and authority today? Is our obedience more important than the results, or do both matter?*

Prayer: Jesus, thank you for healing us and saving us. When you call us to do something, may we be quick to obey.

DAY 24: A MIRACLE MEAL

TODAY'S PASSAGE: MARK 6:34–44, WITH
MATTHEW 14:14–21, LUKE 9:10–17, AND JOHN
6:5–15

Focus verse: *They all ate and were satisfied, and the disciples picked up twelve basketfuls of broken pieces of bread and fish.* (Mark 6:42–43)

Crowds often flock to Jesus, and when they show up, it's an opportunity for him to teach. In today's passage it's a huge crowd. We'll later learn there were five thousand men there, along with women and children. Though it's merely a projection, this enormous crowd could have been anywhere from ten to twenty-five thousand people, perhaps more.

Jesus has compassion on them, for they have no one to lead them. He teaches them many things.

We don't know what he says, but it's a long message that goes late into the day.

His disciples urge him to wrap up and send the people on their way to get something to eat.

Jesus has a different idea. "You feed them," he says.

Their only idea is to go out and buy bread for the crowd, but that would take a lot of money—and time—and doesn't seem like a workable solution.

Jesus refocuses their attention. "What do *you* have?"

They take an inventory. "Five loaves of bread and two fish." And John adds that this food isn't even what the disciples have. It's what a boy offers to share.

For Jesus, five loaves of bread and two fish are enough. He tells the people to sit and prepare to eat. He thanks God for the provisions. Breaking the loaves and fishes into pieces, he gives them to the disciples to pass out.

The disciples do. As they go about their task, the food miraculously multiplies. Everyone has enough to eat and there are even leftovers. They pick up twelve basketfuls of broken fish and bread.

Each of the twelve disciples began with a few pieces of bread and fish, but they end up with much more, effectively one basket each. And we'll witness another mass feeding, this time for four thousand men, along with women and children, in Matthew 15:29–38 and Mark 8:1–8.

In both instances, Jesus miraculously multiplies a small meal to feed thousands of people. Though he could have started with nothing and performed the same miracle just as easily, he doesn't. Instead, he works with what the disciples have.

From a human standpoint, what the disciples had wasn't anywhere close to being enough. But with Jesus it was all he needed.

When it comes to our faith journey, we need to give God what we have and trust him with the rest. Our little, coupled with his power, can produce much.

Questions: *Though it may not seem like a lot to us, what do we have to give to Jesus? How well do we do in trusting God to make up for what we lack?*

Prayer: Heavenly Father, we give you what we have. Multiply it to grow your kingdom.

DAY 25: FAITH AND DOUBT

TODAY'S PASSAGE: MARK 6:46–56, WITH MATTHEW 14:22–33 AND JOHN 6:16–24

Focus verse: *Peter got down out of the boat, walked on the water and came toward Jesus.* (Matthew 14:29)

After the miraculous meal that fed thousands of people, Jesus sends the disciples to cross the lake in a boat. He stays on land to dismiss the crowd. The disciples must wonder how Jesus plans to catch up with them later, but they head out without him.

On the water, the disciples have a tough time. The wind blows against them, so they resort to rowing. They struggle all night. As dawn approaches, Jesus comes to them. He walks on the water. Having never seen anything like this, the disciples freak out. They know a person can't walk on water, so they think they must be seeing a ghost.

Jesus tells them to not be afraid. He climbs in the boat, and the wind dies down. Even though they just witnessed a miraculous meal when Jesus multiplied the five loaves of bread and the two fish, they still don't grasp his supernatural power. This includes the ability to walk on water.

This is the extent of Mark's and John's accounts of the story. But Matthew adds another detail. It seems significant.

In addition to Jesus walking on water, Peter does too. Here's what happened.

Jesus approaches the boat, walking on the water. He tells his disciples not to be afraid. Peter impetuously says, "Jesus, if it's really you, tell me to join you."

"Come," Jesus says.

Peter does just that. He climbs out of the boat and walks toward Jesus.

Peter walks on water! Everything's going fine . . . for a while.

Yet the wind and the waves distract him. He takes his eyes off Jesus and looks at the peril around him. His faith wavers. Why did he ever think he could walk on water? Doubt replaces faith. He sinks.

"Jesus!" Peter cries out. "Save me!"

I imagine Peter flailing his arms at Jesus. Jesus reaches out to his disciple and catches him. "Why is your faith so small?" he asks Peter. "Why did you doubt?"

The pair safely reach the boat and climb inside. The wind stops. All is well.

The disciples who remained in the boat acknowledge Jesus as the Son of God. They worship him. So should we.

Questions: *Are we willing to get out of the boat and take a risk, like Peter? Why are we more apt to criticize Peter for doubting than we are the rest of the disciples for not trying?*

Prayer: Jesus, when you call us to come to you, may we obey in faith regardless of what's happening around us.

DAY 26: THE BREAD OF LIFE
TODAY'S PASSAGE: JOHN 6:25–40

Focus verse: *Jesus declared, "I am the bread of life. Whoever comes to me will never go hungry, and whoever believes in me will never be thirsty."* (John 6:35)

In Day 8, we read that Jesus offered the Samaritan woman living water to drink. Now he wants to feed the people life-giving bread. In the same way we need water to live, we also need food, our daily bread.

Let's review. Jesus teaches and feeds a massive crowd of over 5,000 people, which we covered in Day 24. Jesus's disciples leave, and he walks on water to join them on Day 25.

The next day, the people don't see Jesus and

search for him. They eventually find him on the other side of the lake. Since they watched his disciples leave without him, they ask him how he got there.

He doesn't answer them directly. Instead, he criticizes their intentions. They're not seeking him because of his miraculous power but because he fed them. Their concern is for their physical needs and not their spiritual condition.

"Don't strive for food that spoils," Jesus says, "but work for food that lasts. My food, my daily bread, leads to eternal life."

"What must we do to do the work of God?" the people ask.

"The work of God is to believe in the One God has sent." It's that simple. Jesus doesn't give them an extensive list of things to do. He doesn't even give them a brief list. In fact, the one item he gives them is so easy that it doesn't even seem like work. They merely need to believe.

This confuses the people. They ask for a sign. They've already forgotten the miracle meal where Jesus multiplied the food. Or did they not perceive it as a miracle at all?

Jesus reminds them of God giving the people

manna—bread sent from above—to eat when they were in the desert.

The crowd wants this bread too.

"I am the bread of life," Jesus says. "If you come to me, you'll never go hungry or be thirsty again. Just believe, and you'll live forever."

The message of Jesus is easy: believe in him. All we must do is believe Jesus is the bread we need for life eternal.

Questions: *Do you believe in Jesus, that he's the bread of life? How should we live this out?*

Prayer: Thank you, Lord Jesus, for being the bread of life. May we believe in you now and for the rest of our lives.

DAY 27: JEWS AND GENTILES TOO

TODAY'S PASSAGE: MARK 7:24–30 AND MATTHEW 15:21–28

Focus verse: *Jesus said to her, "Woman, you have great faith! Your request is granted." And her daughter was healed at that moment.* (Matthew 15:28)

J esus travels to the city of Tyre. He enters someone's home. He seeks a private place to rest, but he can't keep his presence a secret. The people track him down.

One person who comes to him for help is a foreign woman. Mark says she is a Greek, born in Syrian Phoenicia, a Syrophoenician. Matthew, however, says she is from Canaan. Yet this minor difference in her background doesn't matter. What matters is that as a non-Jew, the Jewish people view her as a Gentile—a religious outsider.

Jesus's focus is on his own Hebrew people, the Jews. Since this woman is not a Jew, she doesn't fit his target demographic.

Mark writes that Jesus says what the people expect, insinuating he came only to help Jewish people, not foreigners. Matthew's account is more direct, with Jesus saying he was sent *only* for the people of Israel. Either way, she is excluded.

This woman has a little girl with a big issue. The girl is possessed by an impure spirit. The mom begs Jesus to heal her daughter and drive out the demon that controls her.

Jesus dismisses the woman.

As a foreigner, he implies she's a dog, trying to eat the children's food. What he's really doing is creating a teachable moment.

She doesn't back down. His apparent ethnic snub doesn't offend her. She's quick to counter, noting that even the dogs eat the crumbs that fall from the children's table.

Jesus affirms her wise reply, which he proclaims as exemplifying a great faith. He pronounces the little girl healed. When the mother gets home, her daughter is resting in bed. The demon is gone.

Now the people should realize that Jesus came for both Jews and Gentiles. But they don't.

Questions*: When we encounter a roadblock, do we give up or try even harder? When God doesn't seem to listen to our pleas for help, do we stop asking or persist?*

Prayer: Heavenly Father, may we have a strong faith in you, just like this Gentile woman.

DAY 28: JESUS IS THE CHRIST

TODAY'S PASSAGE: MARK 8:27–30, WITH MATTHEW 16:13–20 AND LUKE 9:18–21

Focus verse: *Simon Peter answered, "You are the Messiah, the Son of the living God."* (Matthew 16:16)

J esus asks his disciples a curious question. "Who do people say I am?"

It's a simple question. The disciples don't need to think. Without hesitation, they give him the top three answers:

"Some say you're John the Baptist."

"Others say you are the incarnation of Elijah."

"A third idea is that you're another of the ancient prophets who has come back to life."

They've covered what the people say about

Jesus, though I doubt he really cares what the people think. But he does care what his followers say. It's of critical importance.

Jesus seeks his disciples' perspective. "Now, what do *you* say?" he asks. "Who do you think I am?"

Peter answers first. Though often impetuous, this time his words are profound. "You are the Messiah, whom God promised to send, the Son of God."

Jesus confirms Peter's answer. But he also does something strange. He commands them not to tell anyone. Why would he say this?

If Jesus wants others to hear about the kingdom of God, wouldn't he want his disciples to tell everyone who he is? How can he advance his cause if people hold misconceptions about him being John the Baptist, Elijah, or another prophet who has come back to life? With them thinking these things, it would hamper the truth that he is the Messiah—the Savior of the people—who is the Son of God.

Yet if the word gets out that Jesus is the Son of God, the Romans could view him as a threat and prematurely execute him. Though Jesus knows his death will come, it must happen at a different time.

This may be why he wants his disciples to keep quiet about him being the Son of God.

Matthew, however, adds another detail to this story. It's an intriguing one.

After Peter makes his bold proclamation that Jesus is the Christ, the Son of God, Jesus blesses him for his confident declaration, which the Father supernaturally revealed to him.

"On this rock," Jesus tells Peter, "I will build my church." This has a two-fold meaning.

First, Jesus had already given Simon a new name of Peter. Peter means *rock*. At a basic level, Jesus is telling Peter that he will be the rock, the foundation, for Jesus's church. Peter, who is already emerging as a leader among the disciples, will do just that.

The deeper meaning, however, is that the rock Jesus will build his church upon is Peter's testimony that Jesus is the Messiah, the Son of God.

This truth is the rock-hard foundation of our faith.

Questions: *Who do we say Jesus is? Are we confident enough to tell others?*

Prayer: Jesus, may we boldly tell others you are the Messiah, the Son of the living God.

DAY 29: PICK UP YOUR CROSS

TODAY'S PASSAGE: MARK 8:31–9:1, WITH MATTHEW 16:21–28 AND LUKE 9:22–27

Focus verse: *"Whoever wants to be my disciple must deny themselves and take up their cross and follow me."* (Mark 8:34)

After Peter declares Jesus is the Son of God, the teacher launches into a prophecy. Jesus tells them what lies ahead for him. He'll suffer at the hands of the religious leaders who will reject him. He'll be killed. But after three days, he'll rise from the dead.

Jesus is direct. This isn't a vague insinuation or parable that they might misinterpret. It's plain, and the disciples can't miss it. Peter objects. He pulls

Jesus aside and rebukes him, that is, Peter corrects his Rabbi. At least he starts to.

In like manner, Jesus rebukes Peter. "Get behind me, Satan!"

That's harsh. Is Jesus calling Peter, Satan?

I don't think so, even though that appears to be the case.

Peter's perspective is off. To him, Jesus's death would be the worst thing that could happen. Yet the Father's plan is that Jesus will die as a human sacrifice for his people—a sin sacrifice to end all sacrifices. Then he'll rise from the dead to prove his mastery over it.

Though Jesus looks at Peter when he speaks and appears to address him, I think Jesus is really addressing Satan. It could be that Satan prompted Peter to say what he did to distract Jesus from his mission. Or it could be that Satan is tempting Jesus to follow Peter's suggestion and avoid death—a most painful and gruesome ordeal.

From this we learn that when Satan tempts us, we can address him and tell him to stop. This is one way we can resist the devil (James 4:7).

Jesus says that to truly be his disciple, we must deny ourselves, pick up our cross, and follow him. Luke adds that we are to do this each day.

To deny ourselves means to put Jesus first. And to pick up our cross means to be willing to die for his cause. This doesn't mean we *will* die for Jesus, merely that we must be prepared to. We must put him first.

If we strive to live, we will die. If we live for ourselves, we will lose everything. Yet those who lose their life—either figuratively or literally—for the sake of Jesus and his good news, will ultimately save it.

This idea of picking up our cross to follow Jesus can begin when we tell others about him. If we're ashamed of him and his words, he'll be ashamed of us.

May we never disappoint our Savior.

Questions: *What do you think about directly speaking to Satan? In what ways can we pick up our cross to follow Jesus?*

Prayer: Jesus, give us courage to boldly tell others about you.

DAY 30: JESUS GLOWS

TODAY'S PASSAGE: MARK 9:2–13, WITH
MATTHEW 17:1–13 AND LUKE 9:28–36

Focus verse: *Then a cloud appeared and covered them, and a voice came from the cloud: "This is my Son, whom I love. Listen to him!"* (Mark 9:7)

Our passage from yesterday, Day 29, ends with a curious promise. "Some of you won't die until you first see the kingdom of God." Though we may wonder what this means, we don't need to wait long to find out. About a week later this plays out in a dramatic—and intriguing—fashion.

Jesus takes his inner circle of disciples—Peter, James, and John—with him to a high mountain.

The four of them are alone. He transforms before them. That is, he transfigures. His form and appearance change. Jesus glows.

Each of the three gospel accounts about this event offer different words to explain Jesus's transfiguration. This suggests the writers struggle to find the right words to describe what happened. Or perhaps the transfiguration of Jesus is beyond description.

Mark says that Jesus's clothes become a dazzling white. Matthew adds that Jesus's face shines like the sun. And Luke uses the imagery of being as bright as a flash of lightning.

But there's more. Moses and Elijah appear with Jesus. The three of them have a conversation. I wish the gospel writers had shared the details, but all we know is that they talk with Jesus about his departure from earth and how he will bring fulfillment to Jerusalem. Implicitly Jerusalem means the Jews and, by extension, everyone else.

Overwhelmed, Peter doesn't know what to say, but that doesn't stop him. He suggests building shelters for Jesus, Moses, and Elijah. These may be to protect them from the elements. Or these shelters may be more like monuments to commemorate what happened. Regardless, it's a bad idea, so Peter's reason doesn't matter.

Before Jesus responds to Peter's suggestion, a cloud covers them. A voice emanates from within. It's the voice of God. He says, "This is my Son. I so love him. Listen to him."

This is the second time God affirms Jesus. We covered the first time in Day 2 as Jesus began his ministry. Now we hear it again as Jesus moves closer to completing his mission.

Just as suddenly, the cloud disappears, and Moses and Elijah are gone. It's only Jesus and his three disciples. He tells them to keep this matter to themselves until he rises from the dead. But they still don't understand what he means.

Though they were confused then about Jesus rising from the dead, it's clear to us now. Jesus died to save us from our sins and rose from the dead. If we follow him now, we can also rise from the dead to live with him in heaven for eternity.

Questions*: If Jesus's transfiguration here on earth was so dazzlingly white and bright, what might he be like when we're with him in heaven? How might we be transformed after we die?*

Prayer: Jesus, thank you for dying for us and saving us. May we live a life worthy of your amazing gift.

DAY 31: NOTHING IS IMPOSSIBLE

TODAY'S PASSAGE: MARK 9:14–29, WITH
MATTHEW 17:14–21 AND LUKE 9:37–43

Focus verse: *[Jesus's] disciples asked him privately,*
"Why couldn't we drive it out?" He replied, "This kind can
come out only by prayer." (Mark 9:28–29)

W hen Jesus and his three disciples—
Peter, James, and John—descend
from the mountain after his transfiguration, they come upon a commotion. The other
nine disciples stayed at the bottom of the mountain,
waiting for their master and friends to return.

As they wait, a man brings his son to the disciples and asks them to heal him. The boy is
possessed by a spirit that keeps him from speaking.

The nine disciples try to address the man's

request, but they fail. Though it may surprise us that they even try, remember that Jesus already gave them authority to heal the sick and cast out demons when he sent them in pairs on their first missionary journey. We covered this on Day 23.

The disciples watched Jesus model how to heal the sick and cast out demons. He gave them authority to do so too. And they went out and did it. Surely, they could handle this man's request to heal his son. But they can't.

Because of their failure, a crowd has gathered. The disciples and religious leaders argue.

When they spot Jesus, the people run to him in expectation. Jesus learns what happened and criticizes the people for their unbelief. The father of the boy struggles to believe as well.

Jesus tells him, "All things are possible to those who believe."

The father's delightful response confirms both his faith and his doubt. "I believe. Help me with my unbelief."

Jesus rebukes the impure spirit and commands him to leave the boy. After some drama, the spirit does, and the boy is fine.

When they're alone, the disciples ask Jesus why they couldn't drive the impure spirit from the boy.

Jesus says that situations like that require prayer (and fasting). Matthew, however, includes a different detail that Mark omits. Matthew writes that it was the disciples' lack of faith that kept them from healing the boy.

"Even the tiniest bit of faith will allow you to move mountains," Jesus says. "And nothing will be impossible."

Questions: *Do we have a faith that moves mountains? How does prayer and fasting fit into our work for Jesus—and into our lives?*

Prayer: Jesus, we believe in you. Help us with our unbelief.

DAY 32: THE SPIRITS SUBMIT

TODAY'S PASSAGE: LUKE 10:1–24, WITH MATTHEW 11:20–30

Focus verse: *"However, do not rejoice that the spirits submit to you, but rejoice that your names are written in heaven."* (Luke 10:20)

I n our reading for Day 23 we talked about how Jesus sent out his twelve disciples in pairs to heal people and encourage them to repent. But this isn't the only time he dispatches his followers to spread his good news.

In today's passage, Jesus sends out another group. This one is much larger. It's six times bigger, which means they can cover six times the territory.

This time Jesus sends out seventy-two people, again in pairs. Though the twelve disciples may have been involved in this second missionary endeavor, Luke notes that it's seventy-two *others*. This implies it's a completely different group. They're to serve as Jesus's advanced team to go ahead of him to the various towns he plans to visit.

He gives them some general instructions for their mission, which we'll do well to consider when we send out missionaries today. Specifically, Jesus tells the seventy-two to heal the sick and proclaim the coming kingdom of God.

As Jesus's emissaries, those who listen to the message of salvation are in effect listening to Jesus. And those who reject our words reject Jesus. It's something to keep in mind as we tell others about Jesus. If they reject our message—the good news about Jesus—it's not us they're rejecting but Jesus. It's not about us; it's all about him.

The groups do as Jesus instructs. They return filled with joy. In astonishment, they say that even the demons yielded to them in the name of Jesus. This shows us there is much power in his name.

Jesus shares what he saw in the supernatural realm as they went about their task. "Satan fell like lightning from heaven." This shows how much the work of the seventy-two afflicted the devil. Imagine the collective impact we could have today.

Jesus, however, puts this in perspective for them. Though it's amazing that the spirits submit to them, it isn't the main point. This isn't something they should celebrate. Instead, they should rejoice over their right standing with God and their future in heaven with him.

Our eternal life through Jesus is what matters most, not how much supernatural power we wield.

Questions*: How should we apply the truth that there's power in Jesus's name? What things can we celebrate in our life?*

Prayer: Jesus, when confronting evil, may we recognize the power of your name.

DAY 33: AN UNLIKELY HERO

TODAY'S PASSAGE: LUKE 10:25–37

Focus verse: *He wanted to justify himself, so he asked Jesus, "And who is my neighbor?"* (Luke 10:29)

One day an expert in the law—that is, the Scriptures—comes to Jesus to assess his knowledge. Today we might call this man a theologian or an academic. He has a question for Jesus. Though his question may be sincere, he may also want to demonstrate his superior training or to trip Jesus into saying something damning.

Regardless of his motivation, he asks Jesus, "What must I do to inherit eternal life?"

Jesus answers in the form of a question. "What does Scripture say?"

"Love God with your whole heart, soul, strength, and mind," the religious expert says. "And love your neighbor as much as you love yourself."

Jesus likes the man's answer and tells him to do it.

This is a bigger task than the man wants. He seeks to limit the scope of it, so he asks Jesus what he means by *neighbor*.

Jesus shares a story—a parable—to explain.

Robbers attack a man traveling alone. They strip him, beat him, and leave him to die. Along comes a religious man, a priest. He sees the man but doesn't want to get involved, so he doesn't stop. Next, a Levite approaches. He sees the man and ignores him as well.

Then, a Samaritan man—someone the Jews look down upon—arrives. He sees the injured man and wants to help. At risk to himself, should the robbers return, he treats the man's wounds and takes him to town. He stays with him overnight and the next day pays the innkeeper to watch over the man. The Samaritan also promises to pay any additional expenses that may come up.

At this point, Jesus asks, "Who was the true neighbor to the injured man?"

The religious expert can't even bring himself to say the word *Samaritan*. He simply says that the true neighbor was the one who showed mercy to the man in need.

Jesus tells him to do the same.

Through this parable of the Good Samaritan, we see that anyone in need is our neighbor, and we are to show love to them.

Yet this is only the second part of what the man cited from the Scriptures. And we must not lose sight of the first part. The first half of his answer is that we must love God with our entire self. In doing so, we're best able to love others as much as we love ourselves.

This is what eternal life means.

Questions: *How can we love God more fully? What must we do to be a better neighbor, loving them as much as we love ourselves?*

Prayer: Holy Spirit, show us how to love God more fully and better love our neighbors.

DAY 34: SISTERS IN CONFLICT
TODAY'S PASSAGE: LUKE 10:38–42

Focus verse: *"Lord, don't you care that my sister has left me to do the work by myself? Tell her to help me!"* (Luke 10:40)

After Jesus teaches the expert of the law what it means to be a neighbor, he and his disciples head out and travel to a village. There a woman invites them into her house. Her name is Martha. She has a sister, Mary, and a brother, Lazarus.

In reading what the Bible says about Martha, we can draw several conclusions: She owns her own home. She likes to entertain and has the gift of hospitality. Her love language is acts of service. Given this, she seems like a wonderful woman. And she is. Yet she's not without her shortcomings.

Scripture shares two stories about Martha. Today's passage is the first.

After inviting Jesus and his followers to her home, Martha busies herself in preparing a meal for them. With at least thirteen more people to feed, this is no small task. It's laborious, and Martha struggles.

A peeved Martha complains to Jesus that her sister, Mary, isn't helping prepare the meal. Instead of assisting Martha in the kitchen, Mary is hanging out with Jesus.

In Jesus's surprising response, he affirms Mary as doing the best thing she can do and tells Martha she needs to calm down. This perplexes me, because if Martha followed her sister's example, no one would have anything to eat.

Another consideration, however, is Martha's misguided assumption that Mary should go along with her plans to feed Jesus. It was Martha's choice to invite Jesus over. Mary doesn't make that offer and has no obligation to help. Both sisters show their commitment to Jesus. But they do it differently.

Though we may be quick to criticize Martha for her assumptions, we must balance this with another story about her. This one is in John 11:1–44. We'll cover it in Day 49, but here's a summary:

After her brother, Lazarus, dies, Jesus arrives to comfort Martha and her sister. He promises Martha that Lazarus will rise again. She believes this but assumes it will happen when the world ends.

"I am resurrection and life," Jesus says. "Anyone who believes in me will live, even though they die. Do you believe this, Martha?"

Martha's response provides us with one of the most profound, faith-filled testimonies about Jesus that we find in Scripture: "I believe you're the Messiah, the Son of God, who is to come into the world" (John 11:27).

Her boldness and confidence should inspire us. May this be what we best remember Martha for and not her irritation with her sister for not helping in the kitchen.

May we also agree with Martha that Jesus is the Messiah and the Son of God.

Questions*: How often do we expect others to go along* *with our grand ideas or commitments? What is our testimony about Jesus?*

Prayer: Holy Spirit, reveal to us how we are to best serve Jesus and show him our love.

DAY 35: TEACH US TO PRAY

TODAY'S PASSAGE: MATTHEW 6:5–15 AND
LUKE 11:1–13

Focus verse: *"If you forgive other people when they sin
against you, your heavenly Father will also forgive you."*
(Matthew 6:14)

One day Jesus is praying. He does this a lot. When he finishes, one of his disciples asks him to teach them how to pray. This is a curious question. We can assume they've been praying their entire life. Surely they know how to do it. Yet to ask Jesus to teach them suggests they realize that how they've been taught to pray and how others pray fall short. Their prayers are inadequate, and they want to learn a better way.

Jesus gives them a model of how to pray. We

find this recorded in Luke's biography of Jesus. But most people aren't familiar with this prayer. It's shorter than the version they learned and lacks some familiar phrasing.

There's a different wording to this prayer, which we find in Matthew's biography of Jesus. It's in what we call Jesus's Sermon on the Mount. Jesus gives the shorter version, found in Luke, to his disciples at another time. We shouldn't be concerned that they differ.

Though many people have memorized the version of this prayer as recorded in Matthew and may recite it during church services, we may be better off to consider it as a model to follow. Here are the key elements in it, which we can adapt as appropriate:

- We start by directing our prayer to our Heavenly Father.
- We bless him.
- We ask for his kingdom to come.
- We ask that his will be done here on earth, just as in heaven.
- We request that he provide our daily bread, that is, the things we need for today.

- We seek his forgiveness, in the same way that we forgive others.
- We ask that he keep us from temptation.
- We request that he deliver us from Satan.
- And some copies of this text add a concluding phrase of praise.

In the more concise version from the book of Luke, we see these same elements, except for the phrase about his will being done here on earth and the concluding sentence of praise.

One phrase in both prayers that roll off our tongues is one that most people give little thought to. We ask God to forgive us, just as we have forgiven others.

But what if we haven't forgiven them? What if we're holding back? Does this petition imply that we give God permission to hold back his forgiveness from us? It's a worrisome thought.

To make sure we don't dismiss or misinterpret this part of the prayer, Jesus immediately launches into a teaching about it. He says directly that, if we forgive other people when they sin against us, our Heavenly Father will also forgive us.

The implication is that if we don't forgive

others, he won't forgive us. Though this may be an overstretch—because through Jesus's sacrificial death on the cross, our sins are forgiven—holding onto unforgiveness is a risk we shouldn't take.

Therefore, we should be quick to forgive others, just as Jesus forgave us.

Questions: *Who do we need to forgive? With God's help we can. How can we use this prayer to better inform our own prayers?*

Prayer: Lord Jesus, thank you for teaching us how to pray. May we use this model to guide our daily prayers.

DAY 36: THE GREAT FEAST IN HEAVEN

TODAY'S PASSAGE: LUKE 13:22–30

Focus verse: *"People will come from east and west and north and south, and will take their places at the feast in the kingdom of God."* (Luke 13:29)

One day someone asks Jesus, "Will only a few people be saved?"

As he often does, Jesus answers indirectly. "Make every effort to enter through the narrow door, because many who try to get in will fail."

Jesus gives an example. He talks about a home-owner on the inside and people on the outside pounding to get in. When the owner peeks out, the people beg him to let them in.

"I don't know you," he says.

"Sure, you do," they answer. "We've hung out and told others about you."

The owner shakes his head. "I don't know you, so go away." The man slams the door.

These people wail in distress. The prophets made it in but not them.

The people who expect to enter—who assume it's a sure thing, that they have an inside track—stand rejected on the outside. They shake their heads.

Which side of the door will we be on?

Is getting in going to be easy or hard? Do we think we've done the right things only to find we've fallen short? With our eternal future at risk, how should we react to Jesus's analogy?

Before we panic, keep reading. Jesus adds that people will flock from all directions to take their place on the inside for the enormous feast in God's kingdom.

This is confusing. Will only a few people make it in through the narrow door or will people swarm in to share in a wonderful celebration?

The answer is "Yes."

Consider the context. Jesus's audience is Jews. It's one of them who asks how many will be saved.

Jesus warns the Jews to strive to enter through the narrow door. But it will be easy for the Gentiles—that is, everyone else.

Jesus isn't dismissing God's chosen people. Instead, he warns them to not take their standing with the Father as a sure thing, to not assume they're automatically in. Just going to the synagogue each week and following their religious rules isn't enough.

The teacher adds, "The last will enter first, but the first will enter last." This means that the Gentiles, who were once outsiders, will get in first, and the Jews, who were once insiders, will get in last.

But they will get in. All they need to do is follow Jesus.

Questions: *Who do you think you'll be surprised to see at Jesus's feast in God's kingdom? What should our attitude be toward Jewish people?*

Prayer: Thank you, Jesus, for dying to save us. May your chosen people, the Jews, turn to you and be saved as well.

DAY 37: COUNT THE COST

Focus verse: *"If anyone comes to me and does not hate father and mother, wife and children, brothers and sisters— yes, even their own life—such a person cannot be my disciple."* (Luke 14:26)

Another time, a large crowd travels with Jesus. He tells them what it takes to truly follow him and be his disciple. In doing so, he uses some strong language. He talks about hate.

Jesus says that if we want to be his disciple—a true disciple—we must hate our parents, our spouse, our children, and our siblings. We must even hate our own life. Then he says we should pick up our cross and follow him.

What does he mean about picking up our cross? In Jesus's time, a cross is an instrument of execution. It signifies death. For the people to pick up their cross to follow Jesus shows that they're willing to die for him. That's commitment. And that's what Jesus wants.

Hating our family and dying for Jesus are some huge barriers to grapple with. Does Jesus really want us to hate our family and despise our own life to the point of death before we can fully follow him?

No.

Jesus exaggerates to make his point. He wants disciples who will make him their priority. He wants disciples to consider what it will cost to follow him. They must fully commit.

He shares two short parables to better explain this.

The first is a builder who wants to erect a tower. Before he starts, he figures out the total cost of the project. This will save him embarrassment from starting construction and not having enough money to finish. So, too, when we decide to follow Jesus. We want to finish what we start and not give up partway through. We must finish our race (2 Timothy 4:7).

The second parable is about a king preparing for battle. Won't he first analyze the situation and look at troop strength to determine if he can hope to defeat his enemy? And if he doesn't expect to win, wouldn't he pursue a peaceful solution instead of going to war? In the same way, we need to count the cost before we promise to follow Jesus.

Jesus doesn't want us to be his disciples if we haven't considered what it will take to go all in for him. He's not trying to talk us out of following him, but he does want us to consider what it may cost us to put him first in our lives.

To be fully committed to following him, we must put him first above everyone—and everything —else.

Questions: *Though we may say we put Jesus first, do our actions and attitudes confirm it? What might it cost us to follow him and be his disciples?*

Prayer: Lord Jesus, may we go all in for you and finish our race strong.

DAY 38: LOST AND FOUND

TODAY'S PASSAGE: LUKE 15:1–32, WITH
MATTHEW 18:10–14

Focus verse: *"We had to celebrate and be glad, because this brother of yours was dead and is alive again; he was lost and is found."* (Luke 15:32)

In today's passage, the religious leaders criticize Jesus. This is something they do often. They grumble that he spends time with sinners. Are they implying they think he should spend time with them instead? It's something to consider.

Instead of reacting to their complaint directly, Jesus launches into a parable. A man has one hundred sheep, and one wanders away. Though he could stay home and be happy he still has ninety-nine, he leaves to search for his one lost sheep.

When he finds the wayward sheep, he carries it home. Joy swells within him, and he calls his neighbors to rejoice with him. So it is with our Heavenly Father when one of his sheep repents.

Likewise, Jesus says to consider a woman with ten coins who loses one of them. This is tragic. She's lost 10 percent of her savings, one tenth of her wealth. In a panic, the woman must find the lost coin. She lights a lamp and sweeps the floor—possibly made of dirt—until she finds it. The relieved woman shares her good news with her neighbors. So it is in heaven with one sinner who repents.

Continuing, Jesus gives a third parable, repeating his central message a third time to emphasize his point. This time there's a man with two sons. The younger one disrespects his father by asking for his inheritance before the man dies. The father agrees, and the boy leaves town. He lives wildly and squanders his inheritance. Broken and hungry, he gets a job feeding pigs. His situation is so desperate that even the pig food looks good to him, but no one offers him any.

Realizing his father's hired laborers have plenty

to eat, he heads home, intent on begging for a job with his dad. Yet before he arrives, his father spots him from afar and runs out to greet him. The young man confesses his sin against his dad, but before he can ask for a job, his father decides to throw a lavish party to welcome his lost boy home. This upsets the older brother.

Though we often call this third lesson the parable of the prodigal son or the lost son, a better name would be the story of two sons. We can learn from both boys and what they did.

The point, however, of all three parables is the same. Something—or someone—was lost but later found. A grand celebration ensued.

May we all be found in Jesus . . . and celebrate when others are found.

Questions: *Are you lost, or are you found? How much do we celebrate each time someone repents to follow Jesus?*

Prayer: Jesus, thank you for searching for us when we were lost. And may we marvel at the glorious celebration that occurred when you found us and brought us home.

DAY 39: THANK YOU, JESUS
TODAY'S PASSAGE: LUKE 17:11–19

Focus verse: *He threw himself at Jesus' feet and thanked him.* (Luke 17:16)

L uke tells us a story of Jesus dealing with ten lepers. Leprosy is an infectious skin decease that eats away the flesh. It's treatable today, but that wasn't the case two thousand years ago. At that time, leprosy was a lifetime affliction and could end in premature death. It was also contagious.

The Old Testament law addresses leprosy and other related skin diseases. Those afflicted must live alone, keep their mouths covered, and warn people of their presence by calling out, "Unclean!" (Leviticus 13:45–46).

Though Scripture doesn't specify it, in practicality, the only people lepers can safely live with are other lepers. It may be that these ten lepers lived together, albeit in isolation from everyone else. Regardless, they travel together in this story. They've heard about Jesus's healing power and hope he can help them too.

These ten lepers approach Jesus but keep their distance—as was the requirement and practice of the day. They call out to him for help. "Take pity on us!"

Another requirement of the law was that a person who recovered from leprosy or another skin condition needed to go to a priest for confirmation before re-entering society (Leviticus 13:2–8). Although these ten men still have leprosy, Jesus tells them to go present themselves to the priest as if they have been healed.

With no logical reason to comply, the lepers do what Jesus told them to do. As they go to the priest, they are *cleansed* of their leprosy.

One man—a Samaritan—sees that all signs of his leprosy are gone. He returns to Jesus and thanks the Healer for what he did.

Jesus commends the man but is surprised that only one person returned to say thanks. Luke notes that the man was *made well*.

There seems to be a distinction between being *cleansed* and being *made well*.

One thought is that being cleansed means the leprosy is gone, but its ravages remain, whereas being made well restores the flesh to its pre-leprous condition.

Another thought is that being made well addresses the whole person, encompassing the physical and emotional aspect of being ostracized and devalued as a person.

Whatever the precise meaning, it's clear that the man who gave thanks to Jesus—and didn't take the Healer's generosity for granted—received even more as a result.

Though Jesus doesn't require us to thank him, it's good when we do.

Questions: *When is the last time we thanked Jesus? What can we do to* show *our gratitude?*

Prayer: Thank you, Jesus, for all you've done for us. You saved us and healed us. You made us well.

DAY 40: BE READY

Focus verse: *Jesus replied, "The coming of the kingdom of God is not something that can be observed."* (Luke 17:20)

J esus often teaches about the kingdom of God. Over eighty verses in his four biographies mention the kingdom of God and its synonym, kingdom of heaven.

The Pharisees ask Jesus when the kingdom of God will come. Though Jesus has taught much about this subject, it might not have been to this group. Or maybe it was, but they didn't understand. Regardless, Jesus says, "The kingdom of God is in your midst."

More than a dozen times Jesus proclaims the present reality of the kingdom of God. He says it is near (Luke 10:11) and it is upon you (Luke 11:20). It happened in that generation (Luke 21:32), and some saw it before they died (Luke 9:27; see Day 30).

In his well-known Sermon on the Mount (as covered in Day 14), Jesus tells the people to seek first his kingdom, that is, to seek first the kingdom of God (Matthew 6:33).

These verses all address a present reality for the kingdom of God.

Yet Jesus has an alternate perspective in mind when he addresses this topic to his disciples. To them he talks about the *future* coming of the kingdom of God. This is when he will come again. But to return, he must first leave. When he's away, they'll long to see him.

First, he will suffer much and be rejected by the people.

When he comes back, it will be unexpected. It can't be observed or predicted. Jesus gives two reminders of Old Testament passages to reinforce his point.

The first is of Noah. At God's command, he

builds an ark when there is no apparent reason to do so. Everyone else goes about their business with life continuing as normal. But the rain comes, and everyone dies in the flood—everyone except Noah, his family, and the animals who are safe inside the ark (Genesis 7:23).

The other is of Sodom and Gomorrah. The people go about their normal activities, unaware that destruction is about to occur. They continue to eat and drink, buy and sell, and plant and build. Yet when Lot and his family leave, God destroys everything that's left.

Even Lot's wife doesn't make it. Though she flees the city with her husband and daughters, she looks back at what she's leaving behind. And she dies (Genesis 19:24–26).

In like manner, when Jesus returns, we must be ready and not look away like Lot's wife. When the Savior comes back, two people will be together. One will meet Jesus, and the other will be left behind.

We don't know when this will be, but we must be ready.

PETER DEHAAN

Questions: How ready are we for Jesus to return at any moment? How should we live our lives today knowing that he could come in the next hour--or not until after we die?

Prayer: Lord Jesus, when you return may you find us ready. And until that day, may we faithfully serve you and do your will.

DAY 41: SEEK JUSTICE

TODAY'S PASSAGE: LUKE 18:1–8

Focus verse: *"Will not God bring about justice for his chosen ones, who cry out to him day and night? Will he keep putting them off?"* (Luke 18:7)

Next, Jesus gives a parable to his disciples. It's often called the parable of the persistent widow. The teacher gives them a situation to envision.

There's a town with an indifferent judge. He doesn't fear God. And he doesn't care about the people he's supposed to serve.

The second character in this parable is a widow. In that culture, being a widow suggests she's poor and dismissed. She comes before the judge, pleading for justice against someone who has wronged her.

The judge doesn't care. He refuses to get involved.

Yet she keeps coming before him, day after day, over and over.

Eventually she wears him down. He answers her request and gives her the justice she seeks. But he doesn't do this because it's what's right or because her case has merit. He does it to keep her from bugging him. He helps her because it's in his best interest, not because she deserves it or because it's his job. This shows he's a self-centered, unjust official.

If an unjust judge will eventually do the right thing, how much more will our Heavenly Father—who *is* just—hear our pleas for justice when we call to him day and night? He won't dismiss us. He'll make sure we get the justice we seek.

Luke notes that this is a parable to remind the disciples to always pray and not give up. Yet this parable is for a specific type of prayer, one of seeking justice. Does this mean this is a lesson for all prayers or only prayers for justice?

It may be both.

The specific meaning is that we should not give

up praying for justice. This can be justice for us or justice for others.

A more widespread application, however, is for all prayers of petition. We need only balance this lesson to persist with the requirement to not engage in vain repetition, that is, to think God will hear us through babbling or our many words (Matthew 6:7).

Jesus shares this parable right after teaching the Pharisees about the kingdom of God and his disciples about his return. Is there a connection?

Simply that as we wait, poised for Jesus to come back, we should continue in prayer, faithful till he returns.

Questions: *How can we better pray for justice for those who are oppressed? How can we continue in prayer and also keep our requests fresh?*

Prayer: Holy Spirit, show us people who need justice and remind us to pray for them.

DAY 42: OFFER MERCY

TODAY'S PASSAGE: JOHN 8:2–11

Focus verse: *"No one, sir,"* she said. *"Then neither do I condemn you," Jesus declared. "Go now and leave your life of sin."* (John 8:11)

One time Jesus's detractors drag before him a woman caught in the act of adultery. They do this to test him. They hope to trick him into saying something incriminating, something they can use against him. These religious leaders who present the adulterous woman care nothing for her, what she did, or about justice. They only care about maligning Jesus.

If they have genuine concern for the law they claim to uphold, they should bring her adulterous partner along with her. It takes two to have an affair. According to their law, both deserve to die (Deuteronomy 22:22). But they don't care about the man's role in this.

Instead, they're exploiting the woman. They want to trap Jesus into saying something they can use against him. With their vast knowledge of Scripture and their made-up rules about religion, they're sure they can twist whatever Jesus says to ruin him.

The woman is their pawn. Nothing more.

But Jesus doesn't take sides, something the woman's accusers hadn't considered. Had he upheld the law or offered her mercy, they would have used his words against him. Instead, he thwarts their scheme. Without pronouncing judgment, he says the person without sin may throw the first rock to kill her. No one qualifies. In shame, they slink away.

Once they leave, Jesus offers the woman mercy. He tells her she is free to go and encourages her to change her behavior.

Too often, well-meaning religious leaders are quick to condemn others when they should extend love and encouragement.

But what about the guy? We can only speculate

who he is. It could be he was one of their own, and they wanted to protect him. Another possibility is that this was a setup, that he seduced and trapped the woman with the goal of them catching her in the act so they could drag her before Jesus. Another thought is that their tryst was mutual and ongoing.

Regardless, the religious leaders have a double standard. They accuse the woman of adultery and let the man go, even though he is just as guilty. This reveals the religious leaders' corruption and exposes their agenda.

Jesus didn't condemn the woman. Neither did he condone her actions. Instead, he offered her mercy and encouraged her to change her lifestyle.

Questions*: Is our nature to judge others or to offer them mercy? How can we follow Jesus's example to neither condemn nor condone the sins of others?*

Prayer: Jesus, may we follow your example and not condemn others nor condone the sin in their lives. May we extend mercy and love instead of judgment.

DAY 43: SEE AND BELIEVE

TODAY'S PASSAGE: JOHN 9:1–41

Focus verse: *Then the man said, "Lord, I believe," and he worshiped him.* (John 9:38)

Jesus and his disciples meet a man blind from birth. The disciples assume sin caused his blindness. That's how they view God, that he afflicts people who do wrong, and he punishes them.

This situation, however, confuses the disciples. "Did his parents' sin cause this," they ask, "or the man's sin?"

Jesus's answer surprises them. "Neither." The man's blindness isn't the result of punishment for his sins or his parents'. Instead, it's to show God's power.

Though the man doesn't ask Jesus to heal him, Jesus acts anyway. But he doesn't order the blindness to go away or command the man's sight to return. Instead, Jesus makes a dressing out of dirt and spit, applying the mud he makes to the man's eyes.

Jesus still doesn't proclaim healing. Instead, he tells the man to go to a pool and wash the mud from his eyes. Imagine a blind man walking down the road with mud caked over his eyes.

The man reaches the pool, washes the mud from his face, and sees for the first time. Through Jesus, the man's life forever changes. This is what happens when we do what Jesus says. He's about transforming lives.

Yet, this takes place on the Sabbath, a day the law of Moses says to keep holy and not do any work (Exodus 31:14–15 and Exodus 35:2). To the religious leaders, Jesus healing the man constitutes Sabbath work, which vexes them. So blinded by their narrow perspective, they condemn Jesus for making the man's life better. They call the Healer a sinner. Yes, they claim that Jesus—who comes to save people from their sins—is himself a sinner. They can't see God in front of them and at work.

These religious leaders also attack the man Jesus healed. They insult him. They accuse him of being a disciple of Jesus. The man gives a most insightful declaration. "If Jesus were not from God, he could do nothing."

At that, they throw the once-blind man out.

When Jesus hears this, he searches for the man and encourages him to believe. The man does and worships Jesus.

Jesus says he came into the world so that the blind would see. This applies to physical blindness, as well as spiritual blindness.

Jesus healed the man, and the man sees his need for Jesus and believes. He had been physically blind, and Jesus restored his sight. Now that the man believes in Jesus, he has spiritual sight too.

Yet the Pharisees condemn Jesus for healing on their holy day. They also condemn the formerly blind man for giving glory to God. In doing so, they show they're spiritually blind. They don't believe in Jesus. They can't because they don't see him.

Questions: *How open are we to help others on Sunday? Are there times when we let our traditions impede what Jesus did and what the Bible says?*

Prayer: Jesus, open our eyes so we can see you at work and advance your kingdom, on every day of the week.

DAY 44: ONE FLOCK

TODAY'S PASSAGE: JOHN 10:1–21

Focus verse: *I have other sheep that are not of this sheep pen. I must bring them also. They too will listen to my voice, and there shall be one flock and one shepherd.* (John 10:16)

J esus gives the Pharisees an image to consider. He talks about a sheep pen with a gate. The shepherd goes into the sheep pen through the entrance. He calls his sheep, and they follow him out into the pastures.

Only a thief would sneak into the pen another way. Yet the sheep don't know the robber's voice and won't follow him.

Jesus likens himself to the gate. In this way, he protects his sheep and keeps them safe. He won't let someone with ill intent enter the sheep pen. The thief comes to steal, kill, and destroy. But Jesus comes that they may live a full life. But he isn't talking about sheep at this point. He's talking about us.

Jesus isn't only the gate. He's also the good shepherd.

Though we're familiar with the phrase *good shepherd*, it only occurs three times in the Bible, all in today's passage.

Jesus, as the good shepherd—*our* good shepherd—is caring, protective, and patient. He's also brave, wise, and sacrificial. He knows our names.

As our shepherd, he loves us, watches over us, and rescues us when we get into trouble, which we too often do. As our good shepherd, Jesus is willing to die for his sheep. In fact, he does. He dies to make us right with Father God.

When danger comes, the good shepherd won't run away as a hired man would. He sticks around to protect his sheep.

Yet there's more.

Jesus doesn't only have sheep in this one pen. He has other sheep too. They also listen to his voice and follow him where he takes them. He'll get them and bring all his sheep together so there will be one flock, with one shepherd.

When we follow Jesus as our good shepherd, we must take care to get along with all the other sheep in his flock. This includes both those sheep from our own pen and Jesus's other sheep who have joined us.

We are one flock, with one shepherd. May we never lose sight of this.

Questions: *Do we follow Jesus as our good shepherd? How committed are we to being one flock with all of Jesus's other sheep?*

Prayer: Jesus, may we get along well with all your sheep, especially those who are not from our pen. Thank you for being our good shepherd. You know us, you love us, and you died to save us.

DAY 45: ONE FLESH

TODAY'S PASSAGE: MARK 10:1–12, WITH MATTHEW 19:3–12 AND LUKE 16:18

Focus verse: *"So they are no longer two, but one flesh. Therefore what God has joined together, let no one separate."* (Mark 10:8–9)

As Jesus teaches a crowd of people, some Pharisees approach to ask him a question. This isn't because they care about the answer. It's because they're testing him. They want to trap him into saying something they can use against him. Such is the case with most of the questions the Jewish leaders ask him.

Their question is about divorce. "Is it lawful?"

Jesus refers them to Scripture. "What did Moses say?"

They answer that Moses allowed a man to write a certificate of divorce and send his wife away (Deuteronomy 24:1–4). Yet they misinterpret Moses's intent. The pivotal justification for divorce in this passage is the word *indecency*. But we don't really know what it means. If the woman was guilty of premarital sex or adultery, the law specifies death by stoning, which would make divorce a nonissue. So, indecency means something else. Though we don't know what that is, it certainly doesn't cover whatever the husband deems it to be. Yet that's how the Pharisees interpret the passage.

This gives Jesus the opportunity to talk about marriage and divorce, sharing God's perspective on the subject.

First, God created us as male and female. In his perfect plan there are two genders and no more, regardless of how people try to define it. We are biologically male or biologically female. By our created nature, we are physically attracted to each other and get married, with the man leaving home to unite with his wife. In this way, the two become one flesh. They will be united (Genesis 2:24).

As husband and wife, they have children, fulfilling God's command to be fruitful and multiply (Genesis 9:7). This also biologically ensures the perpetuation of the species. This was God's intent from the beginning of time.

Now, back to the question of divorce. Jesus says that Moses's "certificate of divorce" provision is because of the people's hard hearts, not because of God's intent. Instead, what God has brought together—through their marital, sexual union—let no person separate.

Lest there be any confusion, Jesus later tells his disciples that anyone who divorces and later remarries commits adultery. The idea of them being united as one flesh is a lifelong intent.

In Matthew's account, Jesus adds additional information. The one—and the only—permissible justification for divorce is sexual immorality. Various versions of the Bible use the words fornication, unchastity, unfaithfulness, whoredom, and "some terrible sexual sin," but sexual immorality is the most common phrase (Matthew 19:9).

This is a high standard for marriage, one that too many have lost sight of in today's world. We must reclaim marriage as God intended and as Jesus taught. Divorce is permissible only in cases of sexual immorality and nothing more. We must resist society's reinterpretation of marriage and misuse of divorce.

Married people are one flesh. Except for unfaithfulness, divorce is not an option.

Questions: *How has society's view of easy divorce, for any reason, infiltrated our church? How has it impacted our personal views?*

Prayer: Father God, may we treat marriage as sacred and permanent, just as you planned.

DAY 46: PUT JESUS FIRST

TODAY'S PASSAGE: MARK 10:17–31, WITH
MATTHEW 19:16–30 AND LUKE 18:18–30

Focus verse: *Jesus looked at him and loved him. "One thing you lack," he said. "Go, sell everything you have and give to the poor, and you will have treasure in heaven. Then come, follow me."* (Mark 10:21)

Next, we read the story of a rich man. He asks Jesus an earnest question: "What must I do to inherit eternal life?"

His use of the word *inherit* is interesting—and confusing.

His question implies that salvation is something we can inherit. Is this a misconception of the rich man?

We can't inherit a right relationship with God

from our parents. This is not a condition that is passed on from one generation to another. Instead, it's one we need to seek and receive on our own.

The man's use of the word *inherit*, however, does imply that eternal life is a gift, one given after the death of a benefactor. It's not something we can earn. With our salvation through Jesus, these conclusions are both true: it is a gift, and we inherit it.

We do not earn our future life in heaven; it's given to us. Yes, someone must die before we can receive this inheritance, but in this case it's not a relative. It's Jesus. Jesus dies so that we can have eternal life.

However, when the rich man asks Jesus this question, the Savior hasn't yet died. So, the answer would seem unfinished.

This may be why Jesus starts by reminding the man about six of the Ten Commandments. The man claims to have obeyed all six since he was a child.

Jesus gives him one more requirement. He tells the man to liquify his assets and give all the money to those in need. In doing so, he'll store up treasures in heaven (Matthew 6:19–20).

This saddens the man because he is very

wealthy. He walks away. His money on earth is more important to him than his eternal life in heaven.

During his ministry, many people ask Jesus a form of this same question about eternal life. Interestingly, he gives them different answers. This must depend on their circumstances. His most common answer, however, is "follow me." Sometimes this is accompanied by an act that shows repentance or the command to pick up their cross, as we covered in Day 29. Both are required before they can fully follow him.

As for this man, his wealth is a roadblock that keeps him from following Jesus—and keeps him out of heaven.

Questions: What threatens to get in our way of following Jesus? How can we shift our focus from what we have now in our physical world to what we'll have later in heaven?

Prayer: Thank you, Jesus, for dying for us so we can have eternal life through you.

DAY 47: TWO RESPONSES TO JESUS
TODAY'S PASSAGE: JOHN 10:22–42

Focus verse: *They said, "Though John never performed a sign, all that John said about this man was true." And in that place many believed in Jesus.* (John 10:41–42)

The Jews ask Jesus if he is the Messiah they've been expecting. They want a direct answer.

"I already told you," Jesus says, "but you didn't listen."

The works he does—miracles, healings, and exorcisms—all testify to who he is because he does them in his Father's name. "But you don't believe me because you're not my sheep."

Jesus says his sheep listen for his voice. As good

sheep, they obey what he tells them to do. They follow him and go where he tells them to go. (We first covered this in Day 44).

As our shepherd, he only does what's in our best interest. We should do what he says. As his sheep, Jesus knows us. We follow him. Where he goes, we're right behind him.

"Come here, little sheep," he says. "This path is a better one. It will keep you from danger." We trail behind him—or at least we should.

As Jesus's sheep, he gives us eternal life. Because of him, we'll live forever. Though our physical bodies will one day die, our spiritual beings will not. We'll live with Jesus in heaven for eternity. It seems too good to be true. Through Jesus we will have life forever, and nobody can stop that from happening.

Jesus gives us a promise that no one will ever take us—his sheep—away from him. Nobody will snatch us from his safe embrace and protective care.

But the Jews object to what Jesus says. They don't like that he calls God his Father. It's sacrilegious, so they reject his message and his offer. They're so infuriated that they try to seize him. They want to stone him to death for blasphemy.

But he slips through their grasp. He crosses the

Jordan River and returns to where John the Baptist had earlier been preaching and baptizing.

Many people who had heard John speak are there. They come to Jesus. "Even though John performed no miracles," they say, "everything he said about this man has come true." And many of them believe in Jesus.

Some people hear Jesus's message, and they reject him. Yet others believe.

Questions*: Do we listen to Jesus's voice and follow him like good sheep? How should we react to the eternal life Jesus gives us?*

Prayer: Jesus, thank you for being our good shepherd. You care for us, show us the right path, and give us eternal life.

DAY 48: THE TOP TWO COMMANDS

TODAY'S PASSAGE: MARK 12:28–34 AND
MATTHEW 22:34–40

Focus verse: "'*Love the Lord your God with all your heart and with all your soul and with all your mind.*' *This is the first and greatest commandment. And the second is like it:* '*Love your neighbor as yourself.*'" (Matthew 22:37–39)

The religious leaders, specifically the Sadducees and the Pharisees—who don't normally get along—agree to meet. They both oppose Jesus, so in this regard it makes them allies, even though they hold vastly different theologies about God. They plot how they can put Jesus in his place.

One of them—whom Matthew calls an "expert in the law" and we might call a theologian—poses a question to Jesus. He asks Jesus to define the greatest commandment.

There's a lot for Jesus to pick from. First there are the Ten Commandments. In addition, there are 613 more specific instructions of things to do or not do as found in the law of Moses. Beside those, there are tens of thousands more rules that the religious leaders devised over the centuries to help the people best follow the 613 commands.

Since the man knows the law well and Jesus lacks formal training, the man is sure Jesus will falter in his answer. Once he does, they'll have something to accuse him of that they can use against him to diminish his influence or stop his ministry.

But Jesus has an answer. Not only does he address the man's question, but he also adds to it. His answers comprise the central lesson for us to direct all that we do.

Jesus quotes from Deuteronomy 6:5 and tells the man we are to "Love God as our Lord with all our heart, soul, and mind." Then Jesus confirms it. "This is the most essential commandment. It is the first, and it is the greatest."

Jesus has wisely answered the man's question, but he's not done. He shares the second greatest commandment too. It comes from Leviticus 19:18 and is "to love others as much as we love ourselves."

Jesus adds, "These two commands stand above all else in Scripture, that is, the law and the prophets."

To love God and to love others as much as we love ourselves smartly summarizes Jesus's entire ministry. The first four of the Ten Commandments focus on our relationship with God, while the last six focus on our relationship with others. And each of the 613 commands found in the Torah fits into one of these two categories.

Today we don't need to adhere to a lengthy list of rules with legalistic zeal, like the Pharisees did. We have but two principles to guide us in all that we do. Love God, and love others.

May we do exactly that.

Questions: *How can we love the Lord God more fully? What must we change in our life to love others as much as we love ourselves?*

Prayer: Holy Spirit, show us how we can better love the Lord and the people you created.

DAY 49: JESUS COMFORTS MARTHA

TODAY'S PASSAGE: JOHN 11:17–27

Focus verse: *"Yes, Lord," [Martha] replied, "I believe that you are the Messiah, the Son of God, who is to come into the world."* (John 11:27)

We first covered Martha in Day 34. In that reading we talked about her error of letting her meal preparation distract her from focusing on Jesus. In today's reading we'll talk about her faith and the confidence she has in Jesus. It's a refreshing reversal and shows that our past mistakes need not define our future. Such is true, especially so, when we follow Jesus.

Jesus has a special affinity for Martha and her

siblings, Mary and Lazarus. Lazarus is sick, and the sisters must be really concerned for they send word to Jesus. By the time Jesus arrives, it's too late. Lazarus is dead and buried—for four days.

When the news reaches Martha that Jesus is on his way, she goes out to meet him. With a mixture of criticism and faith, she says, "If only you'd been here, he wouldn't have died." She's confident that Jesus could have healed her brother, but she's upset that he didn't arrive in time to do so.

"But I know God will answer your prayers even now," she adds. This seems like she expects Jesus to raise her brother from the dead.

Jesus assures her. "Lazarus will rise again."

"Yes, I know," Martha answers. "He'll rise again in the resurrection at the end of time."

"I am the resurrection," Jesus says. "All who believe in me will live, even though they die. Do you believe this, Martha?"

"I do," she says. "I believe you're the Messiah, God's Son, who has come into the world." Martha's confident testimony of who Jesus is provides us with an example to emulate. May her faith in Jesus—during a time of profound loss—encourage us to persevere in like manner when difficulties or disappointments befall us.

To prove he is indeed the resurrection, Jesus goes to Lazarus's tomb. He orders the people to move the stone that blocks the entrance. When Martha objects, because of the odor that will gush out, Jesus reminds her to believe.

When the people roll away the stone from Lazarus's grave, Jesus thanks God for hearing his prayer and calls his dead friend to come out of the tomb. Lazarus does.

We're left to wonder what role Martha's faith played in Jesus raising her brother from the dead. May we have that same rising-from-the-dead faith.

Questions: *Does our life show that we believe Jesus is the Son of God? Do we trust that he will resurrect us from the dead so we can live with him forever in heaven?*

Prayer: Jesus, may we place our confidence in you, just like Martha did.

DAY 50: BLESSED IS HE

TODAY'S PASSAGE: MARK 12:38–40, WITH
MATTHEW 23:1–39 AND LUKE 20:45–47

Focus verse: *"For I tell you, you will not see me again until you say, 'Blessed is he who comes in the name of the Lord.'"* (Matthew 23:39)

J esus's ministry on earth winds down. He'll soon accomplish what he came to do. He'll die for our sins in the ultimate sin sacrifice. But that's not all. He'll later rise from the dead to prove his mastery over death. All we need to do is believe and follow him.

He's spent the past three years telling others the good news about the kingdom of God. Some receive his message with gladness and acceptance.

Others—especially the religious leaders—reject him and his words. He represents change, and they don't like it. His existence threatens them and their religious beliefs. They want to kill him and plan to do so.

Jesus warns the people about these religious leaders. Mark and Luke both give a concise summary of his critical words, while Matthew records a lengthy rebuke.

Jesus begins by encouraging the people to do what their religious leaders tell them to do, but they should definitely not follow these leaders' examples. They don't practice what they preach. They place burdens on people but refuse to help them. And they do things for show, to get attention and garner respect.

Don't defer to them by calling them Rabbi or father, Jesus warns. "Those who promote themselves will face humiliation, while the humble will be exalted."

He lists seven woes—or miseries—they cause in the name of their religion. It's a scathing list of hypocrisy and double standards.

Even though they have perverted the Father's intent and rejected his Son, Jesus still cares for them. He longs to gather them like a hen gathers her chicks to protect them beneath her wings, but they aren't interested.

In Matthew's account, Jesus's long rebuke ends with him saying, "I tell you the truth, you won't see me again until you say, 'Blessed is he who comes in the name of the Lord.'"

This is exactly what happens during Jesus's triumphal entry into Jerusalem, which we sometimes call Palm Sunday. It occurs only days before his execution at the hands of his detractors.

Questions: *How quick are we to praise Jesus for coming in the name of the Lord? If you haven't yet believed in Jesus, will you do it now?*

Prayer: Thank you, Jesus, for coming to earth in the name of the Lord to save us and usher in the kingdom of God.

[Though Jesus's ministry nears its end, his mission is far from over. Continue the story in The Passion of Jesus, *a devotional covering the season of Lent.]*

If you liked *The Ministry of Jesus,* please leave a review online. Your review will help others discover this book so they can read it too.

Thank you

HOLIDAY CELEBRATION DEVOTIONALS

Which devotional do you want to read next?

- The Advent of Jesus
- The Passion of Jesus (Lent)
- The Victory of Jesus (Easter)
- Thanksgiving with Jesus
- New Year with Jesus

Be the first to hear about Peter's new books and receive updates at PeterDeHaan.com/updates.

IF YOU'RE NEW TO THE BIBLE

Each entry in this book contains Bible references. These can guide you if you want to learn more. If you're not familiar with the Bible, here's an overview to get you started, give some context, and minimize confusion.

First, the Bible is a collection of works written by various authors over several centuries. Think of the Bible as a diverse anthology of godly communication. It contains historical accounts, poetry, songs, letters of instruction and encouragement, messages from God sent through his representatives, and prophecies.

Most versions of the Bible have sixty-six books grouped into two sections: The Old Testament and the New Testament. The Old Testament contains thirty-nine books that precede and anticipate Jesus. The New Testament includes twenty-seven books and covers Jesus's life and the work of his followers.

The reference notations in the Bible, such as Romans 3:23, are analogous to line numbers in a Shakespearean play. They serve as a study aid. Since the Bible is much longer and more complex than a play, its reference notations are more involved.

As already mentioned, the Bible is an amalgam of books, or sections, such as Genesis, Psalms, or Matthew. These are the names given to them, over time, based on the piece's author, audience, or purpose.

In the 1200s, each book was divided into chapters, such as Acts 2 or Psalm 23. In the 1500s, the chapters were further subdivided into verses, such as John 3:16. Let's use this as an example.

The name of the book (John) appears first, followed by the chapter number (3), a colon, and then the verse number (16). Sometimes called a chapter-verse reference notation, this helps people quickly find a specific text regardless of their version of the Bible.

Although the goal was to place these chapter and verse divisions at logical breaks, they sometimes seem arbitrary. Therefore, it's good practice to read what precedes and follows each passage you're studying. The text before or after it may contain relevant insights into the portion you're exploring.

Here's how to look up a specific passage in the Bible based on its reference: Most Bibles contain a table of contents, which gives the page number for the beginning of each book. Start there. Locate the book you want to read, and turn to that page. Then flip forward to the chapter you want. Last, skim that chapter to locate the specific verse.

If you want to read online, enter the reference into BibleGateway.com or BibleHub.com. Also check out the YouVersion Bible App.

Learn more about the greatest book ever written at ABibleADay.com, which provides a Bible blog, summaries of the books of the Bible, a dictionary of Bible terms, Bible reading plans, and other resources.

ABOUT PETER DEHAAN

Peter DeHaan, PhD, wants to change the world one word at a time. His books and blog posts discuss God, the Bible, and church, geared toward spiritual seekers and church dropouts. Many people feel church has let them down, and Peter seeks to encourage them as they search for a place to belong.

But he's not afraid to ask tough questions or make religious people squirm. He's not trying to be provocative. Instead, he seeks truth, even if it makes people uncomfortable. Peter urges Christians to push past the status quo and reexamine how they practice their faith in every part of their lives.

Peter earned his doctorate, awarded with high distinction, from Trinity College of the Bible and Theological Seminary. He lives with his wife in beautiful Southwest Michigan and wrangles crossword puzzles in his spare time.

A lifelong student of Scripture, Peter wrote the 1,000-page website ABibleADay.com to encourage people to explore the Bible, the greatest book ever written. His popular blog, at PeterDeHaan.com, addresses biblical Christianity to build a faith that matters.

Read his blog, receive his newsletter, and learn more at PeterDeHaan.com.

BOOKS BY PETER DEHAAN

Holiday Celebration Devotionals

The Advent of Jesus

The Passion of Jesus (Lent)

The Victory of Jesus (Easter)

The Ministry of Jesus

Thanksgiving with Jesus

New Year with Jesus

40-Day Bible Study Series

Dear Theophilus (the Gospel of Luke)

Acts Bible Study

Isaiah Bible Study

Minor Prophets Bible Study

Job Bible Study

Living Water (John)

Love Is Patient (1 and 2 Corinthians)

Revelation Bible Study

1, 2, & 3 John Bible Study

Hebrews Bible Study

James and Jude Bible Study

Matthew Bible Study

1 & 2 Peter Bible Study

Mark Bible Study

Bible Character Sketches Series

Women of the Bible

The Friends and Foes of Jesus

Old Testament Sinners and Saints

More Old Testament Sinners and Saints

Heroes and Heavies of the Apocrypha

200 Old Testament Sinners and Saints

Visiting Churches Series

52 Churches

The 52 Churches Workbook

More Than 52 Churches

The More Than 52 Churches Workbook

Visiting Online Church

Other Books

Elephant God

Jesus's Broken Church

Martin Luther's 95 Theses

The Christian Church's LGBTQ Failure

Bridging the Sacred-Secular Divide (formerly *Woodpecker Wars*)

Beyond Psalm 150

How Big Is Your Tent?

For the latest list of all Peter's books, go to PeterDeHaan.com/books.